CIMA Exam Practice Kit

Fundamentals of Business Economics

CIMA Exam Practice Kit

CIMA Certificate in Business Accounting

Fundamentals of Business Economics

Walter Allan

ELSEVIER

Amsterdam • Boston • Heidelberg • London • New York • Oxford
Paris • San Diego • San Francisco • Singapore • Sydney • Tokyo

CIMA Publishing is an imprint of Elsevier
Linacre House, Jordan Hill, Oxford OX2 8DP, UK
30 Corporate Drive, Suite 400, Burlington, MA 01803, USA

First edition 2008

British Library Cataloguing in Publication Data
A catalogue record for this book is available from the British Library

ISBN: 978 18561 7708 5

For information on all CIMA publications
visit our web site at www.books.elsevier.com

Typeset by Integra Software Services Pvt. Ltd, India
Printed and bound in Great Britain

10 11 12 10 9 8 7 6 5 4 3 2 1

Contents

About the Author

Walter Allan is a graduate of Heriot-Watt University and has lectured, written, published and examined in the fields of economics and management for the past 30 years.

He was the first non-Oxbridge graduate to join the teaching staff at Repton School where he wrote his first book in 1983 "Concise A Level Economics".

He has held senior publishing positions with Allen & Unwin, Macmillan and The Institute of Economic Affairs, where he published twelve Nobel Prize winners in Economics.

Today, he is Chief Executive of Galashiels Economic Consultancy, a company which specialises in professional training and his current clients include Cass Business School, London School of Business and Finance, The Institute of Actuaries and Elsevier Publishers.

Syllabus Guidance, Learning Objectives and Verbs

A The Certificate in Business Accounting

The Certificate introduces you to management accounting and gives you the basics of accounting and business. There are five subject areas, which are all tested by computer-based assessment (CBA). The five papers are:

- Fundamentals of Management Accounting
- Fundamentals of Financial Accounting
- Fundamentals of Business Mathematics
- Fundamentals of Business Economics
- Fundamentals of Ethics, Corporate Governance and Business Law

The Certificate is both a qualification in its own right and an entry route to the next stage in CIMA's examination structure.

The examination structure after the Certificate comprises:

- Managerial Level
- Strategic Level
- Test of Professional Competence (an Exam Based on a Case Study).

B Aims of the syllabus

The aims of the syllabus are

- to provide for the Institute, together with the practical experience requirements, an adequate basis for assuring society that those admitted to membership are competent to act as management accountants for entities, whether in manufacturing, commercial or service organisations, in the public or private sectors of the economy;
- to enable the Institute to examine whether prospective members have an adequate knowledge, understanding and mastery of the stated body of knowledge and skills;
- to complement the Institute's practical experience and skills development requirements.

C Study weightings

A percentage weighting is shown against each topic in the syllabus. This is intended as a guide to the proportion of study time each topic requires.

All topics in the syllabus must be studied, since any single examination question may examine more than one topic, or carry a higher proportion of marks than the percentage study time suggested.

The weightings *do not* specify the number of marks that will be allocated to topics in the examination.

D Learning outcomes

Each topic within the syllabus contains a list of learning outcomes, which should be read in conjunction with the knowledge content for the syllabus. A learning outcome has two main purposes:

1 to define the skill or ability that a well-prepared candidate should be able to exhibit in the examination;
2 to demonstrate the approach likely to be taken by examiners in examination questions.

The learning outcomes are part of a hierarchy of learning objectives. The verbs used at the beginning of each learning outcome relate to a specific learning objective, e.g. Evaluate alternative approaches to budgeting.

The verb 'evaluate' indicates a high-level learning objective. As learning objectives are hierarchical, it is expected that at this level students will have knowledge of different budgeting systems and methodologies and be able to apply them.

A list of the learning objectives and the verbs that appear in the syllabus learning outcomes and examinations follows.

Learning objectives	*Verbs used*	*Definition*
1 **Knowledge**		
What you are expected to know	List	Make a list of
	State	Express, fully or clearly, the details of/facts of
	Define	Give the exact meaning of
2 **Comprehension**		
What you are expected to understand	Describe	Communicate the key features of
	Distinguish	Highlight the differences between
	Explain	Make clear or intelligible/State the meaning of
	Identify	Recognise, establish or select after consideration
	Illustrate	Use an example to describe or explain something

Level	Verbs	Definition
3 **Application** *How you are expected to apply your knowledge*	Apply	To put to practical use
	Calculate/compute	To ascertain or reckon mathematically
	Demonstrate	To prove with certainty or to exhibit by practical means
	Prepare	To make or get ready for use
	Reconcile	To make or prove consistent/compatible
	Solve	Find an answer to
	Tabulate	Arrange in a table
4 **Analysis** *How you are expected to analyse the detail of what you have learned*	Analyse	Examine in detail the structure of
	Categorise	Place into a defined class or division
	Compare and contrast	Show the similarities and/or differences between
	Construct	To build up or compile
	Discuss	To examine in detail by argument
	Interpret	To translate into intelligible or familiar terms
	Produce	To create or bring into existence
5 **Evaluation** *How you are expected to use your learning to evaluate, make decisions or recommendations*	Advise	To counsel, inform or notify
	Evaluate	To appraise or assess the value of
	Recommend	To advise on a course of action

Computer-based assessment

CIMA has introduced computer-based assessment (CBA) for all subjects at Certificate level. The website (www.cimaglobal.com/students/admin/assessment/computer/questions.htm) says

> Objective questions are used. The most common type is 'multiple choice', where you have to choose the correct answer from a list of possible answers, but there are a variety of other objective question types that can be used within the system. These include true/false questions, matching pairs of text and graphic, sequencing and ranking, labelling diagrams and single and multiple numeric entry.
>
> Candidates answer the questions by either pointing and clicking the mouse, moving objects around the screen, typing numbers, or a combination of these responses. Try our online demo at [www.cimaglobal.com] to get a feel for how the technology will work.
>
> The CBA system can ensure that a wide range of the syllabus is assessed, as a pre-determined number of questions from each syllabus area (dependent upon the syllabus weighting for that particular area) are selected in each assessment.

There are two types of questions which were previously involved in objective testing in paper-based exams and which are not at present possible in a CBA. The actual drawing of graphs and charts is not yet possible. Equally there will be no questions calling for comments to be written by students. Charts and interpretations remain on many syllabi and will be examined at Certificate level but using other methods.

For further CBA practice, CIMA Publishing is producing CIMA esuccess CD-ROMs for all certificate level subjects. These products are available at www.cimapublishing.com.

Fundamentals of Business Economics

Syllabus outline

The syllabus comprises:

Topic and study weighting

A	The Goals and Decisions of Organisations	20%
B	The Market System and the Competitive Process	30%
C	The Financial System	20%
D	The Macroeconomic Context of Business	30%

Learning aims

This syllabus aims to test student's ability to:

- Distinguish the differing goals of organisations and identify how these differing goals affect the decisions made by managers;
- Illustrate how market economies function and identify the reasons for and impacts of government involvement in economic activities;
- Identify the role of financial institutions and markets in the provision of short- and long-term finance to individuals, businesses and governmental organisations;
- Identify how macroeconomic variables and government economic policies affect the organisation.

Assessment strategy

There will be a computer-based assessment of 2 hours duration, comprising 75 compulsory questions, each with one or more parts.

A variety of objective test question styles and types will be used within the assessment.

Learning outcomes and indicative syllabus content

A The Goals and Decisions of Organisations – 20%

Learning outcomes

On completion of their studies students should be able to:

- distinguish the goals of profit-seeking organisations, not-for-profit organisations and governmental organisations;
- compute the point of profit maximisation for a single product firm in the short run;

- distinguish the likely behaviour of a firm's unit costs in the short run and in the long run;
- illustrate the effects of long-run cost behaviour on prices, the size of the organisation and the number of competitors in the industry;
- illustrate shareholder wealth, the variables affecting shareholder wealth and its application in management decision making;
- identify stakeholders and their likely impact on the goals of not-for-profit organisations and the decisions of the management of not-for-profit organisations (NPOs);
- distinguish between the potential objectives of management and those of shareholders, and the effects of this
- principal–agent problem on decisions concerning price, output and growth of the firm.
- describe the main mechanisms to improve corporate governance in profit-seeking organisations.

Indicative syllabus content

- The forms of ownership of organisations by which we mean public, private and mutual, and their goals.
- Graphical treatment of short-run cost and revenue behaviour as output increases (total revenue and total cost curves) and identification of point of short-run profit maximisation using graphical techniques and from data.
- Long-run cost behaviour and the impact of economies and diseconomies of scale.
- Concept of returns to shareholder investment in the short run (ROCE and EPS) and long run (NPV of free cash flows) leading to the need for firms to provide rates of return to shareholders at least equal to the firm's cost of capital.
- Calculation of impact on the value of shares of a change to a company's forecast cash flows or required rate.

Note: Calculations required will be either perpetual annuity valuations with constant annual free cash flows, or NPV calculations with variable cash flows over three years.

- Types of not-for-profit organisations and the status of economic considerations as constraints rather than primary objectives in the long run.
- Role of stakeholders in setting goals and influencing decisions in not-for-profit organisations and potential ways of resolving differing stakeholder demands.
- The principal–agent problem, its likely effect on decision-making in profit-seeking and not-for-profit organisations, and the concepts of scrutiny and corporate governance.

B The Market System and the Competitive Process – 30%

Learning outcomes

On completion of their studies students should be able to:

- identify the equilibrium price in a product or factor markets likely to result from specified changes in conditions of demand or supply;
- calculate the price elasticity of demand and the price elasticity of supply;
- identify the effects of price elasticity of demand on a firm's revenue following a change in prices;
- explain market concentration and the factors giving rise to differing levels of concentration between markets;
- explain market failures, their effects on prices, efficiency of market operation and economic welfare, and the likely responses of government to these;
- distinguish the nature of competition in different market structures;
- identify the impacts of the different forms of competition on prices and profitability.

Indicative syllabus content

- The price mechanism: determinants of supply and demand and their interaction to form and change equilibrium price.
- The price elasticity of demand and its effect on firms' revenues and pricing decisions.
- The price elasticity of supply and its impact on prices, supply and buyers' expenditure.
- Business integration: mergers, vertical integration and conglomerates.
- Calculation of market concentration and its impact on efficiency, innovation and competitive behaviour.
- Impact of monopolies and collusive practices on prices and output and role of competition policy in regulating this.
- Factors causing instability of prices in primary goods markets (i.e. periodic and short-run inelasticity of supply, the cobweb or hog cycle) and the implications of this for producer incomes, industry stability and supply and government policies to combat this (e.g. deficiency payments, set-aside, subsidies).
- Impact of minimum price (minimum wages) and maximum price policies in goods and factor markets.
- Positive and negative externalities in goods markets and government policies to deal with these (including indirect taxes, subsidies, polluter pays policies and regulation).
- Public assurance of access to public goods, healthcare, education and housing.
- Public versus private provision of services (nationalisation, privatisation, contracting out, public private partnerships).

C The Financial System – 20%

Learning outcomes

On completion of their studies students should be able to:

- identify the factors leading to liquidity surpluses and deficits in the short, medium and long run in households, firms and governments;
- explain the role of various financial assets, markets and institutions in assisting organisations to manage their liquidity position and to provide an economic return to holders of liquidity;
- explain the role of insurance markets in the facilitation of the economic transfer and bearing of risk for households, firms and governments;
- identify the role of the foreign exchange market and the factors influencing it, in setting exchange rates and in helping organisations finance international trade and investment;
- explain the role of national and international governmental organisations in regulating and influencing the financial system, and the likely impact of their policy instruments on businesses.

Indicative syllabus content

- The causes of short term, medium term and long term lack of synchronisation between payments and receipts in households (i.e. month-to-month cash flow, short-term saving and borrowing, and longer-term property purchases and pensions provision).
- The causes of short term, medium term and long term lack of synchronisation between payments and receipts in firms (i.e. month-to-month cash flow management, finance of working capital and short-term assets and long-term permanent capital).
- The causes of short term, medium term and long term lack of synchronisation between payments and receipts in governmental organisations (i.e. month-to-month cash flow management, finance of public projects and long-term management of the national debt).

- The principal contracts and assets issued by financial institutions and borrowers to attract liquidity in the short, medium and long term (e.g. credit agreements, mortgages, bills of exchange, bonds, certificates of deposit and equities).
- The roles and functions of financial intermediaries and the principal institutions and markets in the financial system.
- The influence of commercial banks on the supply of liquidity to the financial system through their activities in credit creation.
- Yield on financial instruments (i.e. bill rate, running yield on bonds, net dividend yield on equity), relation between rates, role of risk and the yield curve.
- Influence of central banks on yield rates through market activity and as providers of liquidity to the financial system.
- Principal insurance contracts available and basic operation of insurance markets including terminology (e.g. broking, underwriting, reinsurance).
- The role of foreign exchange markets in facilitating international trade and in determining the exchange rate.
- Effect of exchange rates on the international competitiveness of firms, including elementary foreign exchange translation calculations.
- Credit and foreign exchange risks of international trading firms and the use of letters of credit, export credit guarantees and exchange rate hedging to manage these risks.
- Influences on exchange rates: interest rates, inflation rates, trade balance, currency speculation.
- Governmental and international policies on exchange rates (i.e. exchange rate management, fixed and floating rate systems, single currency zones) and the implications of these policies for international business.

D The Macroeconomic Context of Business – 30%

Learning outcomes

On completion of their studies students should be able to:

- explain macroeconomic phenomena, including growth, inflation, unemployment, demand management and supply-side policies;
- explain the main measures and indicators of a country's economic performance and the problems of using these to assess the wealth and commercial potential of a country;
- explain the stages of the trade cycle, its causes and consequences, and discuss the business impacts of potential policy responses of government to each stage;
- explain the main principles of public finance (i.e. deficit financing, forms of taxation) and macroeconomic policy;
- explain the concept of the balance of payments and its implications for business and for government policy;
- identify the main elements of national policy with respect to trade, including protectionism, trade agreements and trading blocks;
- identify the conditions and policies necessary for economic growth in traditional, industrial and post-industrial societies, and the potential consequences of such growth;
- explain the concept and consequences of globalisation for businesses and national economies;
- identify the major institutions promoting global trade and development, and their respective roles.

Indicative syllabus content

- National Income Accounting identity and the three approaches to calculation and presentation of national income (Output, Expenditure and Income).
- Interpretation of national income accounting information for purposes of time series or cross-sectional evaluation of economic performance.
- The circular flow of income and the main injections and withdrawals.
- Illustration of changes to equilibrium level of national income using aggregate demand and supply analysis.
- Government macroeconomic policy goals (low unemployment, inflation, external equilibrium and growth) and the effects on business of the government's pursuit of these.
- Types and consequences of unemployment, inflation and balance of payments deficits.
- The trade cycle and the implications for unemployment, inflation and trade balance of each stage (recession, depression, recovery, boom).
- Government policy for each stage of the business cycle and the implications of each policy for business.
- The central government budget and forms of direct and indirect taxation. Incidence of taxation (progressive, regressive) and potential impact of high taxation on incentives and avoidance.
- Fiscal, monetary and supply-side policies, including relative merits of each.
- Layout of balance of payments accounts and the causes and effects of fundamental imbalances in the balance of payments.
- Arguments for and against free trade and policies to encourage free trade (e.g. bi-lateral trade agreements, multi-lateral agreements, free trade areas, economic communities and economic unions), and protectionist instruments (tariffs, quotas, administrative controls, embargoes)
- Principal institutions encouraging international trade (e.g. WTO/GATT, EU, G8)
- Nature of globalisation and factors driving it (e.g. improved communications, political realignments, growth of global industries and institutions, cost differentials).
- Impacts of globalisation (e.g. industrial relocation, emergence of growth markets, enhanced competition, cross-national business alliances and mergers, widening economic divisions between countries).
- Role of major institutions (e.g. World Bank, International Monetary Fund, European Bank) in fostering international development and economic stabilisation.

Examination Techniques

Computer-based examinations

Ten Golden Rules

1. Make sure you are familiar with the software before you start the exam. You cannot speak to invigilator once you have started.
2. These exam practice kits give you plenty of exam style questions to practice.
3. Attempt all questions, there is no negative marking.
4. Double check your answer before you put in the final alternative.
5. In multiple choice questions, there is only one correct answer.
6. Not all questions will be MCQs – you may have to fill in missing words or figures.
7. Identify the easy questions first, get some points on the board to build up your confidence.
8. Try and allow five minutes at the end to check your answers and make any corrections.
9. If you do not know the answer try process of elimination. Sadly there is no phone a friend!
10. Take scrap paper, pen and calculator with you. Work out answer on paper first if it is easier for you.

The Goals and Decisions of Organisations

Scarce Resources

Scarce Resources 1

Concepts and definitions questions

1.1 Fill in the blanks

(i) Economics is the study of the creation and distribution of ________.
(ii) The fundamental problem in economics is the allocation of ________ resources.
(iii) Where costs of using resources are minimised, this is known as ________ efficiency.
(iv) Where resources are allocated to meet as many needs of the society as possible, we have ________ efficiency.
(v) The benefit forgone by not using a resource in the next best alternative is known as ________ cost.
(vi) An economy where all decisions are taken by the state is known as a ________ economy.
(vii) An economy where all decisions are taken by individuals is known as the ________ ________ economy.
(viii) An economy which demonstrates some characteristics of a command economy and a free market economy is known as a ________ economy.
(ix) Goods from the consumption of which the benefit derived for one consumer is not at the expense of the benefit for others are known as ________ goods.
(x) There would be an underprovision if a ________ good is left purely to market prices.

1.2 *The production possibility curve*

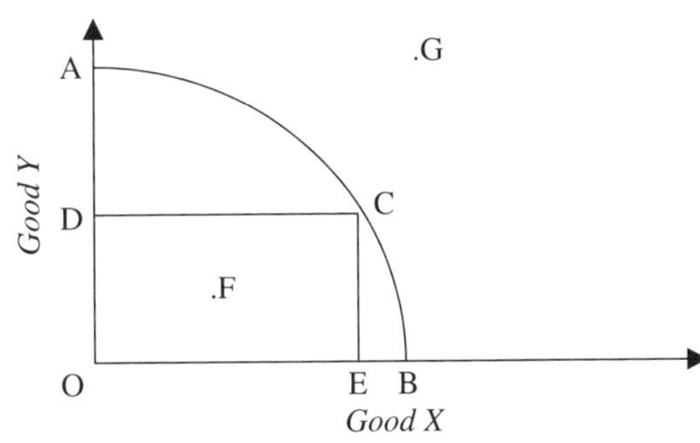

The curve AB defines the productive capacity of the country.

(i) Which point on the diagram is not attainable?
(ii) Which point on the diagram represents underutilised resources?
(iii) Which point on the diagram gives an example of full employment?
(iv) What is the opportunity cost of producing OE units of good X?

1.3 State three advantages of a centrally planned economy.

(i)
(ii)
(iii)

1.4 State three disadvantages of a centrally planned economy.

(i)
(ii)
(iii)

1.5 State four advantages of a free market economy.

(i)
(ii)
(iii)
(iv)

1.6 State four disadvantages of a free market economy.

(i)
(ii)
(iii)
(iv)

1.7

Factors of production	*Reward*
land	interest
labour	profit
capital	wages
enterprise	rent

Select the appropriate reward that goes with the appropriate factor of production.

(i) interest and ________.
(ii) profit and ________.
(iii) wages and ________.
(iv) rent and ________.

1.8 Welfare economics is the study of how resources can be used to maximise the welfare of society. It can be measured in three ways.

(i) ________ efficiency
(ii) ________ efficiency
(iii) ________ efficiency

1.9 Economic growth brings about an increase in the output of an economy leading to an increase in living standards. Write down six conditions likely to promote economic growth.

(i)
(ii)
(iii)
(iv)
(v)
(vi)

1.10 In recent years, there has been a number of economists and others arguing against economic growth. State three valid arguments against economic growth.

(i)
(ii)
(iii)

✓ Concepts and definitions solutions

1.1 (i) wealth
(ii) scarce
(iii) technical
(iv) allocative
(v) opportunity
(vi) command
(vii) free market
(viii) mixed
(ix) public
(x) merit

1.2 (i) G
(ii) F
(iii) C
(iv) AD units of good Y

1.3 (i) no unemployment
(ii) basic needs catered for
(iii) weaker members of society catered for

1.4 (i) lack of incentives
(ii) existence of black markets
(iii) organisations become too bureaucratic

1.5 (i) system responds to consumer preferences
(ii) people have freedom of choice
(iii) competition ensures technical efficiency
(iv) consumers ensure there is allocative efficiency

1.6 (i) unequal distribution of income and wealth
(ii) no supply of public and merit goods
(iii) unemployment
(iv) social costs

1.7 (i) capital
(ii) enterprise
(iii) labour
(iv) land

1.8 (i) productive
(ii) technical
(iii) allocative

1.9 (i) technology
(ii) flexible and educated workforce
(iii) investment in infrastructure
(iv) availability of capital
(v) political stability
(vi) good working environment

1.10 (i) not sustainable if it is based on consumption of finite resources
(ii) causes pollution and environmental damage
(iii) global dominance by large multinationals

Multiple choice questions

1.1 In economics, 'the central economic problem' means that:

A consumers do not have as much money as they would wish
B there will always be a certain level of unemployment
C resources are not always allocated in an optimum way
D output is restricted to the limited availability of resources

1.2 In a market economy, the allocation of resources between different productive activities is determined mainly by:

A the decisions of the government
B the wealth of entrepreneurs
C the pattern of consumer expenditure
D the supply of factors of production

1.3 The economy of the UK is best described as a

A command economy
B free market economy
C mixed economy
D socialist economy

1.4 The opportunity cost to the government of building a new school is

A the money spent on the construction of the school
B the traffic congestion caused during the construction of the school
C the value of goods and services that could otherwise have been produced with the resources used to build the school
D none of the above

1.5 Which of the following is necessarily held constant when drawing the short-run production function?

A the population
B the rate of interest
C the money supply
D the capital stock

1.6 In a market economy, the price system provides all of the following except

A a means of allocating scarce resources
B a signal to consumers
C a signal to producers
D an equal distribution of income and wealth

1.7 Which one of the following is not a social cost?

A passive smoking
B pollution
C traffic congestion
D the National Health Service

1.8 Which of the following is most likely to lead to a fall in a country's productive capacity?

A an increase in technology
B a fall in the population

C the abolition of maximum hours laws
D an increase in retirement age

1.9 Whether we live in a market, mixed or planned economy, the central economic problem is

(i) what to produce
(ii) how to produce
(iii) how to distribute

A (i) and (ii)
B (i) and (iii)
C (ii) and (iii)
D (i), (ii) and (iii)

1.10 Which one of the following is the best measure of the standard of living in a country?

A the amount of savings in the banking system
B the average weekly wage
C gross national product per head
D none of the above

✓ Multiple choice solutions

1.1 **D**

1.2 **C**

In a market economy, producers in the search of profits must respond to consumer demand. Thus the allocation of resources reflects consumer preferences as expressed in their expenditure.

1.3 **C**

Mixed economy

1.4 **C**

Alternative foregone

1.5 **D**

The capital stock

1.6 **D**

A market economy does not provide an even distribution of income and wealth.

1.7 **D**

The NHS – because this is a merit good.

1.8 **B**

A fall in population will reduce a country's productive capacity.

1.9 **D**

So all of the above

1.10 **C**

Gross national product per head

The Business Organisation

The Business Organisation

2

Concepts and definitions questions

2.1 State three constraints likely to be faced by an organisation.

2.2 What is a principal–agent problem?

2.3 Apart from profit maximisation, state three other possible company objectives.

2.4 Give four examples of not-for-profit organisations.

2.5 What are the 3Es?

✓ Concepts and definitions solutions

2.1 (i) The law
(ii) The nature of the business
(iii) Human nature

2.2 A principal–agent problem emerges when the shareholders, that is principals, contract another party, that is managers or agents, to carry out tasks on their behalf. Thus, the objectives of the business may be determined by the agents.

2.3 (i) Sales maximisation
(ii) Satisficing
(iii) Market share

2.4 (i) A charity
(ii) Local government
(iii) A social club
(iv) A regulatory body

2.5 (i) Economy
(ii) Efficiency
(iii) Effectiveness

? Multiple choice questions

2.1 A public company's line of business is determined by its

A Articles of association
B Memorandum of association
C Board of directors
D None of the above

2.2 A company which operates a policy of satisficing is

A Attempting to maximise profits
B Attempting to maximise sales revenue
C Attempting to maximise market share
D Attempting to seek acceptable levels of attainment for various stakeholder groups

2.3 Which of the following would be an example of a merit good?

(i) Health
(ii) Education
(iii) Road Congestion

A (i)
B (ii)
C (iii)
D (i) and (ii)

2.4 Which of the following statements is correct?

A Not-for-profit organisations are only found in the public sector
B Not-for-profit organisations are only found in the private sector
C Not-for-profit organisations can be found in both the public and the private sector
D Not-for-profit organisations cannot survive without profits

2.5 Which of the following are used to measure how well the public sector performs?

(i) Economy
(ii) Efficiency
(iii) Effectiveness
(iv) Elegance

A (i), (ii)
B (ii), (iii)
C (i), (iv)
D (i), (ii), (iii)

✓ Multiple choice solutions

2.1 **B**

A public company's line of business is determined by its memorandum of association.

2.2 **D**

A company which operates a policy of satisficing is trying to keep everybody concerned happy.

2.3 **D**

Health and education are examples of merit goods since they are available to the consumer below market price. Road congestion is an example of a social cost.

2.4 **C**

Not-for-profit organisations can be found in both sectors, for example private sector charity and public sector local authority.

2.5 **D**

Known as the 3Es – economy, efficiency and effectiveness.

Costs, Revenue and Profit

Costs, Revenue and Profit

3

? Concepts and definitions questions

3.1 Fill in the blanks

(i) The ________ run is the time period during which at least one factor of production remains fixed.
(ii) In the ________ run all factors of production are variable.
(iii) ________ costs do not vary in total as the level of output increases.
(iv) ________ costs vary in total in direct relation to changes in the level of output.
(v) ________ cost is the cost of producing one more unit.
(vi) ________ cost is the cost per unit and equals total cost divided by output.
(vii) ________ ________ cost falls as production rises.
(viii) ________ revenue is the extra revenue derived by selling one more unit.
(ix) Fixed cost + variable cost = ________ cost.
(x) Average fixed cost + average variable cost = ________ cost.

3.2 Complete the following table from your knowledge of microeconomic theory and the information given below.

Quantity	Price	Total revenue	Marginal revenue	Fixed cost	Variable cost	Total cost	Average fixed cost	Average variable cost	Average total cost	Marginal cost	Profit
0	–					200					
1	180					250					
2	170					300					
3	160					350					
4	150					400					
5	140					450					
6	130					500					
7	120					550					
8	110					600					
9	100					650					
10	90					700					

3.3 The following data refers to the costs of Firm A and the demand for its product.

Quantity	*Price*	*Total cost*
0	–	20
1	45	35
2	40	45
3	35	60
4	30	90

Using your knowledge of economic theory and the table above

(i) The marginal cost of producing the second unit is ________.
(ii) The extra revenue derived from selling the fourth unit is ________.
(iii) The average fixed cost of the second unit is ________ .
(iv) Profits will be maximised at an output of ________.

3.4 State whether the following statements are true or false.

(i) Profit is maximised where marginal cost is equal to marginal revenue.
(ii) Total revenue is maximised where average cost equals marginal cost.
(iii) Average cost is minimised where marginal cost equals average cost.
(iv) Fixed cost rises as output rises.
(v) Economies of scale will result in the cost per unit falling.
(vi) In the short run, firms will continue to operate provided they cover variable cost.
(vii) Total revenue is maximised when marginal revenue = 0.
(viii) The average cost includes a small amount of profit.

Concepts and definitions solutions

3.1 (i) short
(ii) long
(iii) fixed
(iv) variable
(v) marginal
(vi) average
(vii) average fixed
(viii) marginal
(ix) total
(x) average

3.2

Quantity	Price	Total revenue	Marginal revenue	Fixed cost	Variable cost	Total cost	Average fixed cost	Average variable cost	Average total cost	Marginal cost	Profit
0	–	–	–	200	–	200	–	–	–	–	−200
1	180	180	180	200	50	250	200	50	250	50	−70
2	170	340	160	200	100	300	100	50	150	50	40
3	160	480	140	200	150	350	66.6	50	116.6	50	130
4	150	600	120	200	200	400	50	50	100	50	200
5	140	700	100	200	250	450	40	50	90	50	250
6	130	780	80	200	300	500	33.3	50	83.33	50	280
7	120	840	60	200	350	550	28.5	50	78.5	50	290
8	110	880	40	200	400	600	25	50	75	50	280
9	100	900	20	200	450	650	22.2	50	72.2	50	250
10	90	900	–	200	500	700	20	50	70	50	200

Quantity: Given

Price: Given

Total revenue (TR): TR = quantity × price
TR at 1 = 1 × 180
so TR at 2 = 2 × 170 and so on.

Marginal revenue: The extra revenue is derived from selling one more unit using the formula

Marginal revenue = TR at n − TR at (n − 1)

To find the marginal revenue of the 5th unit take $n = 5$ and $n - 1 = 4$
Therefore, TR at 5 − TR at 4 = 700 − 600
so extra revenue derived by selling 5th unit = 100

Fixed cost: Can be found in two ways.
Fixed cost + variable cost = total cost
However, we have two unknown variables.

The other method is
Fixed cost = total cost at zero output
so 200
This is 200 at every level of output.

Variable cost	Now we have two known variables. If fixed cost + variable cost = total cost, then variable cost = total cost − fixed cost, so at output 1 250 − 200 = 50
Total cost (TC)	Given
Average fixed cost (AFC)	$\text{AFC} = \frac{\text{fixed cost}}{\text{output}}$ so at output 1, $\text{AFC} = \frac{200}{1} = 200$ at output 10, $\frac{200}{10} = 20$
Average variable cost (AVC)	$\text{AVC} = \frac{\text{variable cost}}{\text{output}}$ so at 10 units, variable cost = 500 so average variable cost = 50
Average total cost	$\text{Average total cost} = \frac{\text{TC}}{\text{output}}$ It can also be calculated by adding the two previous columns AFC + AVC
Marginal cost	Cost of producing one more output using the formula TC at n − TC at $(n - 1)$ To find the marginal cost of the 5th unit take $n = 5$ and $n - 1 = 4$ Therefore, TC at 5 − TC at 4 = 450 − 400 so extra cost of selling one more unit is 50
Profit	Difference between total revenue and total cost. If TR > TC, then we have profit If TC > TR, then we have loss.

3.3 (i) 10
(ii) 15
(iii) 10
(iv) 3

3.4 (i) True
(ii) False
(iii) True
(iv) False
(v) True
(vi) True
(vii) True
(viii) True

Multiple choice questions

3.1 The table below shows the relevant costs of a firm at various outputs.

Production	*Total cost*
0	£100
1	£120
2	£140
3	£160
4	£180
5	£200

The average fixed cost of producing 5 units is

A £20
B £100
C £120
D £200

3.2 Diminishing returns occur in the short run because

A one factor of production is fixed
B all factors are variable in the long run
C of diminishing marginal utility
D profits remain constant as output rises

3.3 Cost per unit is minimised where

A marginal cost = average revenue
B marginal cost = average cost
C average revenue = average cost
D marginal revenue = 0

3.4 Diseconomies of scale occur when

A long run average costs begin to rise
B long run average costs begin to fall
C short run average costs begin to rise
D short run average costs begin to fall

3.5 Marginal cost is best defined as

A fixed costs − variable costs
B fixed costs + variable costs
C costs which are of a minor nature
D the change in total costs when output rises by one unit

3.6 Total revenue will be maximised where

A marginal cost = marginal revenue
B marginal revenue = average revenue
C marginal revenue = 0
D marginal cost = variable cost

3.7 Which of the following always rise when a manufacturing business raises output?

(i) total costs
(ii) total variable costs
(iii) fixed costs
(iv) marginal costs

A (i)
B (i) and (ii)
C (i), (iii) and (iv)
D (i), (ii), (iii) and (iv)

3.8 A business which satisfices will

A try to maximise profits
B try to maximise sales
C try to minimise unit cost
D try to achieve a target which is acceptable to all parties

3.9 Which of the following is not a function of profit in a market economy?

A a signal to producers
B a signal to consumers
C a return on capital
D a reward for taking risks

3.10 If a firm is enjoying economies of scale, then

A it is suffering from excess capacity
B it must be a monopoly
C it is maximising profits
D unit cost is falling as output rises

Multiple choice solutions

3.1 **A**

$$\text{Average fixed cost} = \frac{\text{Fixed cost}}{Q}$$

Fixed cost = Total cost at zero

so $\frac{£100}{5} = £20$

3.2 **A**

Diminishing returns occur in the short run because one factor of production is fixed.

3.3 **B**

Cost per unit is minimised where marginal cost = average cost.

3.4 **A**

Diseconomies of scale occur when long run average costs begin to rise.

3.5 **D**

Marginal cost is best defined as the change in total costs when output rises by one unit so $TC^{n} - TC^{n-1}$.

3.6 **C**

Total revenue will be maximised where marginal revenue = 0.

3.7 **B**

Total costs and total variable costs will rise, fixed costs will remain constant, marginal costs could rise or fall.

3.8 **D**

A business which satisfices will try to achieve a target which is acceptable to all parties.

3.9 **B**

A function of profit is a signal to producers not consumers.

3.10 **D**

If a firm is enjoying economies of scale, then unit cost is falling as output rises.

Shareholder Wealth

Shareholder Wealth

4

? Concepts and definitions questions

4.1 State four factors of production.

4.2 How are the following measures of financial performance calculated?

- (i) Return on capital employed
- (ii) Return on net assets
- (iii) Earnings per share
- (iv) Price/earnings ratio

4.3 The technique used to calculate costs and revenues in the future is known as?

4.4 What two elements of return might a shareholder expect from investing in a company?

4.5 State five factors which could affect the price of a share.

✓ Concepts and definitions solutions

4.1 (i) Land
(ii) Labour
(iii) Capital
(iv) Entrepreneurship

4.2 (i) $\text{ROCE} = \dfrac{\text{Profit before interest and tax}}{\text{Average capital employed}} \times 100$

(ii) $\text{Return on net assets} = \dfrac{\text{Operating profit (before interest and tax)}}{\text{Total assets} - \text{current liabilities}} \times 100$

(iii) $\text{EPS} = \dfrac{\text{Earnings per share}}{\text{Market price of share}} \times 100$

(iv) $\text{P/E ratio} = \dfrac{\text{Current market price of share}}{\text{EPS at the last publication of results}}$

4.3 Discounted cash flow technique

4.4 (i) Dividend
(ii) Rise in market share price

4.5 (i) Profits
(ii) Speculation
(iii) Merger/takeover
(iv) Recession
(v) Interest rates

Multiple choice questions

4.1 Over the past year the share price of X plc has increased from 120p to 150p. A dividend of 12p has also been paid. During the year the investor earned a rate of return of

A 15%
B 20%
C 30%
D 35%

The next four questions are based on the following information.

Dividend per share – 8.6p
Net profit after taxation – £17,000
Interest paid – £2,000
Number of ordinary shares – 70,000
Market price of share – 204p

4.2 The dividend yield is

A 8.6%
B 6.4%
C 4.2%
D 2.1%

4.3 The dividend cover is

A 3
B 2.5
C 2
D 1

4.4 The earnings per share is

A 15p
B 18.5p
C 19.7p
D 21.4p

4.5 The price/earnings ratio is

A 10
B 9.5
C 8
D 6

4.6 A company has a share capital of £1million, made up of 2 million 50p shares. If last year's earnings were £2 million and the company had a P/E ratio of 12p, shares should be currently trading for

A 50p
B £6
C £12
D £20

4.7 Interest cover is calculated by dividing what figure by the interest paid?

A Profit before interest and tax
B Profit before interest but after tax
C Profit after interest but before tax
D Profit after interest and tax

4.8 An individual is expecting an income stream of £10,000 over the next four years. If a discount rate of 10% is to be applied, the level of income in Year 4 should be worth

A £9,090
B £8,260
C £7,510
D £6,830

4.9 If the central bank raised interest rates, the most likely outcome on the stock market would be?

A A rise in share prices
B A fall in share prices
C No change in share prices
D Impossible to tell

4.10 A credit card company charges me 3.5% interest per month. If I had a balance at the beginning of the year of £100 and did not make any payments during the year, how much interest would the credit card company charge me?

A £150
B £100
C £51.11
D £42

Multiple choice solutions

4.1 **D**

Dividend	$\frac{12}{120}$	10%
Capital gain	$\frac{30}{120}$	25%
		35%

4.2 **C**

$$\frac{8.6}{204} \times 100 = 4.2\%$$

4.3 **B**

$$\frac{£17{,}000 - £2{,}000}{£6{,}000} = 2.5$$

4.4 **D**

$$\text{EPS} = \frac{£15{,}000}{70{,}000} \times 100 = 21.4$$

4.5 **B**

$$\text{PE} = \frac{204}{21.4} = 9.5$$

4.6 **C**

Price per share = EPS × P/E ratio = 1 × 12 = £12

4.7 **A**

Interest cover is calculated by dividing profit before interest and tax.

4.8 **D**

$$\frac{£10{,}000}{(1.1)^4} = £6{,}830$$

4.9 **B**

Share prices are likely to fall because an increase in interest will raise borrowing costs which will affect profit.

4.10 **C**

At the end of the period the amount owed would be

$£100 \times (1 + 0.035)^{12}$
$= £151.11$

of which £51.11 is interest

Corporate Governance

Corporate Governance

5

Concepts and definitions questions

5.1 Corporate governance is?

5.2 State three roles of shareholders in a company.

5.3 State four key responsibilities placed on the directors of the company.

5.4 How can shareholders lose control of a company they own?

5.5 State three advantages of share option schemes.

5.6 What was the Cadbury Report?

5.7 State five recommendations of the Cadbury Report.

5.8 Write a short definition of:

(i) The Greenbury Report
(ii) The Nolan Committee
(iii) The Hempel Committee
(iv) The Higgs Report

5.9 What is the combined code?

5.10 Write down four features of a good corporate governance model.

✓ Concepts and definitions solutions

5.1 The system by which companies and other organisations are directed and controlled.

5.2
(i) Appoint the directors of the company
(ii) Appoint the auditors for the company
(iii) Assure themselves that the system of governance is appropriate and effective

5.3
(i) To determine the broad long-term aims of the company
(ii) To provide a focus of leadership
(iii) To supervise the management of the company
(iv) To report to shareholders on the performance of the company

5.4
(i) Organisations become too large.
(ii) Organisations become too complex.
(iii) Individual shareholders have minority interest.

5.5
(i) Managers are paid on a performance-related basis.
(ii) Managers take a longer-term view of the organisation's strategy.
(iii) Goal congruence with other shareholders.

5.6 It was based on a committee set up by the Stock Exchange because of the concern over corporate governance. The task of the committee chaired by Sir Adrian Cadbury was to review the process of corporate governance in the U.K.

5.7
(i) Board of directors should meet on a regular basis.
(ii) Directors should have limited period contracts (3 year).
(iii) Greater involvement of non-executive directors.
(iv) Directors reward to be publicly disclosed.
(v) Statement made in annual report stating whether company adheres to Cadbury Report recommendations.

5.8
(i) Greenbury Report – a review of directors' pay
(ii) Nolan Committee – a review of corporate governance in the public sector
(iii) Hempel Committee – a review of general corporate governance issues
(iv) Higgs Report – a review of company board members covering age, gender, skills and abilities

5.9 The combined code is basically a review of all corporate governance issues which have been raised since the Cadbury Committee. They believe the way forward is for companies to pursue a policy of "best practice".

5.10
(i) Separation of power especially the role of chairman and chief executive.
(ii) An appropriate balance of executive and non-executive directors.
(iii) The adoption of the principles of transparency, openness and fairness.
(iv) To ensure that the board of directors are fully accountable.

? Multiple choice questions

5.1 The directors of a company are appointed by

A The shareholders
B Fellow directors
C Non-executive directors
D Auditors

5.2 The non-executive director is appointed by

A The executive directors
B The non-executive directors
C Shareholders
D The chief executive

5.3 Which of the following is not an advantage of share options?

A Managers are paid on a performance basis
B Managers are more likely to take a longer-term view of strategy
C Goal congruence with the shareholders
D Directors will be able to practice insider dealing

5.4 The first attempt at reviewing corporate governance in the UK was the setting up of the Cadbury Committee. This was at the prompting of

A The government
B The Stock Exchange
C The accountancy profession
D The Institute of Directors

5.5 The committee set up to review corporate governance in the public sector was known as the

A Cadbury Committee
B Nolan Committee
C Hempel Committee
D Combined Code of Practice

✓ Multiple choice solutions

5.1 **A**

Directors are appointed by shareholders.

5.2 **A**

The non-executive director is appointed by the executive directors.

5.3 **D**

Directors practising insider dealing is not an advantage since it is illegal.

5.4 **B**

The Cadbury Committee was set up by the Stock Exchange.

5.5 **B**

The committee formed to review corporate governance in the public sector was the Nolan Committee.

Part 2

The Market System and the Competitive Process

Consumer Behaviour and Demand

Consumer Behaviour and Demand

6

Concepts and definitions questions

6.1 Fill in the blanks

(i) Utility theory assumes that consumers wish to maximise ________ ________.
(ii) The extra benefit derived by consuming one more unit is known as ________ ________.
(iii) When a consumer buys more of a good, his total utility rises but each successive increase in utility is less than the previous one. This is known as ________ ________ ________.
(iv) When consumers buy more of one good and less of another because of the relative price changes, this is known as the ________ effect.
(v) For a normal good the substitution effect is reinforced by the ________ effect.
(vi) When a consumer's income rises and the demand for a certain good falls, the good is known as an ________ good.
(vii) When the income effect is negative and this outweighs the positive substitution effect, the good becomes a ________ good.
(viii) Giffen goods have an ________ sloping demand curve.
(ix) The difference between what a consumer is prepared to pay for a good and the market price is known as ________ ________.
(x) The difference between what a producer is prepared to sell a good for and the market price is known as ________ ________.

6.2 *Price elasticity of demand*

(i) Price elasticity of demand (PED) is calculated by ________.
(ii) (a) A perfectly inelastic demand curve would have a coefficient value of ________.
(b) A relatively inelastic demand curve would have a coefficient value between ________ and ________.
(c) A unit elasticity demand curve would have a coefficient value of ________.
(d) A relatively elastic demand curve would have a coefficient value between ________ and ________.
(e) A perfectly elastic demand curve would have a coefficient value of ______.

(iii) The five factors which determine price elasticity of demand are
1
2
3
4
5

6.3 *Income elasticity of demand*

(i) Income elasticity of demand (IED) is calculated by ________.
(ii) An inferior good has a ________ income elasticity of demand.
(iii) A basic or necessity good has an elasticity of between ________ and ________.
(iv) A luxury good has an elasticity greater than ________.

6.4 *Cross elasticity of demand*

(i) Cross elasticity of demand (CED) is calculated by ________.
(ii) A complementary good would have a ________ cross elasticity of demand.
(iii) A substitute would have a ________ cross elasticity of demand.
(iv) A close substitute would have a ________ ________ cross elasticity of demand.
(v) An unrelated product would have a ________ cross elasticity of demand.

6.5 Shifts in the demand curve are caused by

(i)
(ii)
(iii)
(iv)
(v)

Concepts and definitions solutions

6.1 (i) economic welfare
(ii) marginal utility
(iii) diminishing marginal utility
(iv) substitution
(v) income
(vi) inferior
(vii) Giffen
(viii) upward
(ix) consumer surplus
(x) producer surplus

6.2 (i) $\dfrac{\text{\% change in quantity demanded}}{\text{\% change in price}}$
(ii) (a) zero
(b) zero and −1
(c) −1
(d) −1 and infinity
(e) infinity
(iii) 1 availability of substitutes
2 proportion of income spent
3 frequency of purchase
4 nature of the good
5 amount of brand loyalty

6.3 (i) $\dfrac{\text{\% change in quantity demanded}}{\text{\% change in income}}$
(ii) negative
(iii) zero and one
(iv) one

6.4 (i) $\dfrac{\text{\% change in quantity demanded good A}}{\text{\% change in price good B}}$
(ii) negative
(iii) positive
(iv) high positive
(v) zero

6.5 (i) change in consumers' incomes
(ii) change in price of substitute good
(iii) change in price of complementary good
(iv) change in consumers' tastes
(v) successful advertising campaign

? Multiple choice questions

6.1 From the demand schedule below, the price elasticity of demand following a fall in price from 25 to 20p is

Price	*Quantity*
30	15
25	20
20	25
15	30

A −1
B −1.25
C −1.50
D −1.75

6.2 Cross elasticity of demand for good A with regard to good B is

A $\dfrac{\text{\% change in quantity demanded of good B}}{\text{\% change in price of good A}}$

B $\dfrac{\text{\% change in quantity demanded of good A}}{\text{\% change in quantity demanded of good B}}$

C $\dfrac{\text{\% change in quantity demanded of good A}}{\text{\% change in price of good B}}$

D impossible to define cross elasticity without any figures

6.3 Mr Biley earns £100,000 per annum and spends £1,000 per month on housing. His salary rises to £110,000 per annum and he decides to move to a larger house where he pays £1,500 per month on housing. His income elasticity of demand for housing is

A 1
B 2
C 4
D 5

6.4 Following the reduction in price of a normal good there will be

A a positive income and a positive substitution effect
B a positive income and a negative substitution effect
C a negative income effect and a positive substitution effect
D a negative income effect and a negative substitution effect

6.5 A Giffen good is

A a good where demand rises as income rises
B a good where demand rises as income falls
C a good where demand rises as price rises
D a good where demand rises as price falls

6.6 Which of the following is not held constant when we draw the demand curve?

A the price of complementary goods
B the price of substitutes
C consumers' income
D the price of the good

6.7 A student has £5 to spend each week in the school tuck shop which sells biscuits and lemonade. His marginal utility schedule is given below.

Quantity bought	*Marginal utility of lemonade*	*Marginal utility of biscuits*
5	110	90
6	100	75
7	90	60
8	80	50
9	70	40

If lemonade costs 50p and biscuits cost 25p, which combination gives him the greatest utility?

	Lemonade	*Biscuits*
A	7	9
B	8	5
C	9	9
D	6	8

6.8 Consumer surplus is

A the difference between marginal cost and marginal revenue
B the utility gained by consuming one more unit
C the difference between what consumers are willing to pay and the market price
D the tax consumers pay on goods and services

6.9 Gin, whisky and tonic water are assumed to be normal goods. If the price of gin remained constant while the price of whisky falls and tonic rises, what would happen to the sale of gin?

A stay the same
B increase
C decrease
D remain constant if price changes were equal

6.10 If the price of a good fell by 20% but total expenditure on the good remained the same, the demand curve could be described as

A perfectly elastic
B elastic
C perfectly inelastic
D unitary elasticity

Multiple choice solutions

6.1 **B**

Elasticity of demand

$$= \frac{\text{\% change in quantity demanded}}{\text{\% change in price}}$$

$$= \frac{+25\%}{-20\%} = -1.25$$

6.2 **C**

Cross elasticity of demand for good A with regard to good B is

$$= \frac{\text{\% change in quantity demanded for good A}}{\text{\% change in price of good B}}$$

6.3 **D**

Income elasticity of demand

$$= \frac{\text{\% change in quantity demanded}}{\text{\% change in income}}$$

$$= \frac{50\%}{10\%} = 5$$

6.4 **A**

Following the reduction in price of a normal good there will be a positive income and a positive substitution effect.

The income effect comes about because the consumer feels better off and the substitution effect arises because the good now becomes more attractive relative to others.

6.5 **C**

A Giffen good is a good where demand rises as price rises.

6.6 **D**

The price of the good itself is not held constant when we draw the demand curve.

6.7 **D**

The combination which gives the greatest utility is where

$$\frac{\text{marginal utility of good A}}{\text{price of good A}} = \frac{\text{marginal utility of good B}}{\text{price of good B}}$$

so $\frac{100}{50} = \frac{50}{25}$

6 lemonade 8 biscuits

6.8 **C**

Consumer surplus is the difference between what consumers are willing to pay and the market price.

6.9 **C**

Sales would fall because price of complementary good rises and substitute good falls.

6.10 **D**

If total expenditure remains the same we have unitary elasticity.

7 Supply and the Market

Supply and the Market

7

Concepts and definitions questions

7.1 Fill in the blanks

(i) In traditional theory where average cost AC includes normal profit the AC is ________ shaped in the short run.
(ii) In a perfectly competitive market average revenue = ________.
(iii) To maximise profits, firms will produce where ________ cost is equal to ________ revenue.
(iv) In the short run, firms will continue to supply providing they cover ______ costs.
(v) In the long run, ________ costs must be covered.
(vi) In the long run, the supply curve is determined by the ________ cost.

7.2 *Elasticity of supply*

(i) Elasticity of supply may be calculated using the formula ________.
(ii) Factors which affect elasticity of supply include
1
2
3
4
5

7.3 State three factors which would shift a supply curve to the left.

(i)
(ii)
(iii)

7.4 State three factors which would shift a supply curve to the right.

(i)
(ii)
(iii)

7.5 What is the difference between short run and long run in economics?

Concepts and definitions solutions

7.1 (i) U
(ii) marginal revenue
(iii) marginal, marginal
(iv) variable
(v) total
(vi) marginal

7.2 (i) $\frac{\%\text{ change in quantity supplied}}{\%\text{ change in price}}$
(ii) 1 the nature of the product
2 availability of other factors
3 government taxation
4 the level of capacity
5 the time scale

7.3 (i) an increase in expenditure tax
(ii) a rise in costs
(iii) a rise in the price of imported raw materials

7.4 (i) a government subsidy
(ii) an increase in technology
(iii) a reduction in the price of imported raw materials

7.5 The short run is the time it takes to adjust one factor of production and in the long run all factors of production are variable.

Multiple choice questions

7.1 A profit-maximising oil producer discovers that the government is to raise an extra 10% levy on his profits. In order to maintain profit maximisation, which policy would you recommend to him?

A leave price and output the same
B raise price by 10% and raise output by 10%
C lower price by 10% and raise output by 10%
D lower price by 10% and lower output by 10%

7.2 If a firm attempts to maximise profits, it will produce where

A marginal cost = average cost
B marginal cost = 0
C marginal cost = average revenue
D marginal cost = marginal revenue

7.3 In the short run, a firm can continue to operate provided they can cover

A fixed costs
B marginal costs
C average costs
D variable costs

7.4 Which of the following would not shift the supply curve to the right?

A a government subsidy
B a government expenditure tax
C an increase in technology
D lower input prices

7.5 A farmer produces 1,000 tonnes of wheat with the government guaranteeing £50 per tonne produced. If the subsidy is increased by £5 per tonne and production rises to 1,200 tonnes, the elasticity of supply of wheat is equal to

A −1
B +1
C −2
D +2

✓ Multiple choice solutions

7.1 **A**

Regardless of the level of taxation, the profit maximisation level remains the same, just 10% less, so leave price and output the same.

7.2 **D**

Profit maximisation takes place where marginal cost = marginal revenue.

7.3 **D**

In the short run, a firm can continue to operate provided they can cover variable costs.

7.4 **B**

A government subsidy, an increase in technology and lower input prices would all shift the supply curve to the right, a government expenditure tax would shift to the left.

7.5 **D**

$$\text{Elasticity of supply} = \frac{\%\text{ change in quantity supplied}}{\%\text{ change in price}}$$

so $$\frac{+20\%}{+10\%} = +2$$

Price and Output Determination

Price and Output Determination

8

Concepts and definitions questions

8.1 Fill in the blanks

(i) The internal price set for sale within a multinational organisation is the ________ price.
(ii) The exchange value which is determined by supply and demand is the ________ price.
(iii) The market price of a good or service in relation to others is the ________ price.
(iv) Inflation raises all prices but the ________ value may not have risen.

8.2 *Demand and supply*

(i) If demand exceeds supply at a given price there is said to exist ________ demand.
(ii) If supply exceeds demand at a given price there is said to exist ________ supply.
(iii) If demand is equal to supply there is said to exist ________ ________.

8.3 (i) Give a reason why the imposition of a minimum wage might cause unemployment.
(ii) Give a reason why the imposition of a minimum wage might reduce unemployment.

8.4 *Minimum prices*

An agricultural market sells 1,000 sheep at a price of £50 per sheep. By means of a diagram explain the impact on price and quantity sold if the government set a minimum price of £65 per sheep.

8.5 *Maximum prices*

The market clearing price for the rent of a two bed apartment is £500 per month. If the government imposes a maximum price of £400 per month, by means of a diagram show the impact on price and quantity of apartments now being rented.

Concepts and definitions solutions

8.1 (i) transfer
(ii) market
(iii) clearing
(iv) real

8.2 (i) excess
(ii) excess
(iii) market equilibrium

8.3 (i) It raises the wage above the equilibrium price and thus the demand for labour contracts and the supply of labour extends.
(ii) It could reduce voluntary unemployment since it increases the difference between minimum wage and state benefit.

8.4 Demand and supply of sheep

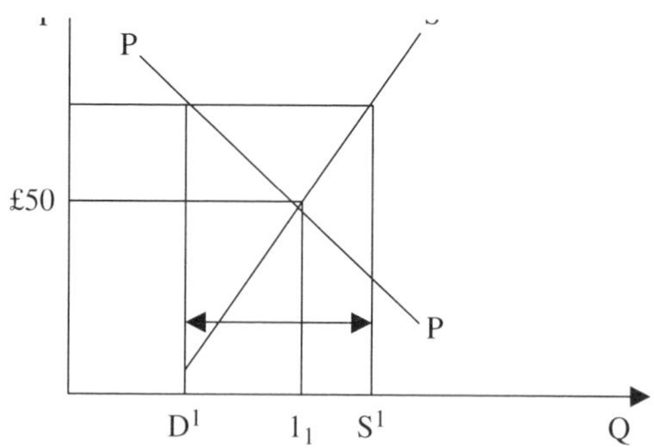

By setting a minimum price above market clearing price, there will be an excess supply of D^1S^1.

8.5 Demand and supply of rented accommodation

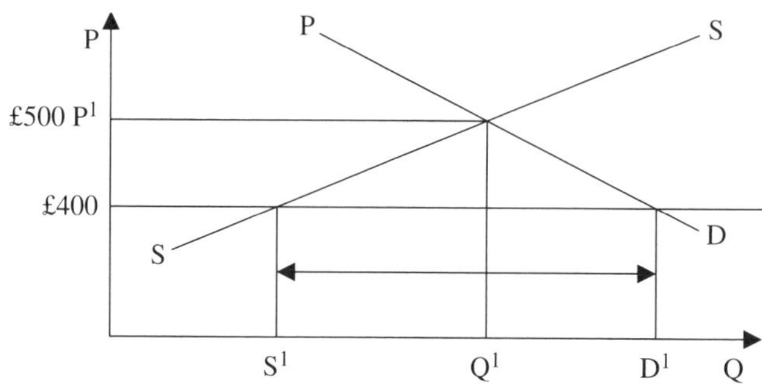

By setting a maximum price below the market clearing price, the government creates an excess demand of S^1D^1.

? Multiple choice questions

8.1 An internal price set for sale within a multinational organisation so that profits are highest in the lowest tax country is known as

A the market price
B the relative price
C the transfer price
D the real price

8.2 The supply of agricultural products in the short run is

A completely elastic
B elastic
C inelastic
D impossible to determine

8.3 A business employs 10 workers at a wage rate of £300. To attract one more worker, wages rise to £330. The marginal cost of the 11th worker would be

A £30
B £300
C £330
D £630

8.4 If the government set a maximum price below the market equilibrium price this will lead to

A excess demand
B excess supply
C market equilibrium
D none of the above

8.5 In the Common Agricultural Policy in order to reduce the butter mountains, a system of what kind was introduced?

A tariffs
B export subsidies
C quotas
D taxes

✓ Multiple choice solutions

8.1 **C**

An internal price set for sale within a multinational organisation is known as the transfer price.

8.2 **C**

The supply of agricultural products in the short run is inelastic.

8.3 **D**

£330	for 11th worker
+£300	£30 increase for other 10 workers
£630	

8.4 **A**

This will lead to excess demand.
See Question 8.5 in Concepts and definitions for proof.

8.5 **C**

A system of quotas was introduced to reduce supply.

9

Large Scale Production

Large Scale Production

9

Concepts and definitions questions

9.1 Fill in the blanks

(i) The level of output on the long run average total cost curve at which average costs first reach their minimum point is known as the __________ __________ __________.

(ii) A reduction in long-term average total cost is known as __________ __________ __________.

(iii) A rise in long-term average total cost is known as __________ __________ __________.

(iv) When a company introduces new products, this is known as __________.

(v) A __________ is a combination of two companies on roughly equal terms with the consent of both parties.

(vi) A __________ is a combination of two companies, where one company acquires the other, sometimes against the wishes of the company which has been acquired.

(vii) A merger between two motor manufacturing companies is an example of __________ integration.

(viii) A merger between a textile manufacturer and a retail clothes shop is an example of __________ integration.

(ix) A merger between a construction company and a tobacco company is a __________ merger.

(x) If a supermarket acquires a farm, this is an example of vertical integration __________.

9.2 State five internal economies of scale which could arise if two large motor manufacturing companies merged.

(i)
(ii)
(iii)
(iv)
(v)

9.3 State three internal diseconomies of scale which could arise if two large motor manufacturing companies merged.

(i)
(ii)
(iii)

9.4 Production may be classified into three categories. They are

(i)
(ii)
(iii)

9.5 State three valid economic arguments in favour of a horizontal merger.

(i)
(ii)
(iii)

9.6 State three valid economic arguments in favour of a vertical merger (forwards or backwards).

(i)
(ii)
(iii)

9.7 Give two reasons why a merger between two companies in different industries would be beneficial to the new company.

(i)
(ii)

9.8 State two advantages and two disadvantages of specialisation.

Advantages

(i)
(ii)

Disadvantages

(i)
(ii)

9.9 Value for Money (VFM) is considered to be the best combination of services from the least amount of resources taking into account the 3Es. What or who are the 3Es?

(i)
(ii)
(iii)

9.10 State four reasons why conflict could exist between managers and shareholders in a company.

(i)
(ii)
(iii)
(iv)

✓ Concepts and definitions solutions

9.1 (i) minimum efficient scale (MES)
(ii) economies of scale
(iii) diseconomies of scale
(iv) diversification
(v) merger
(vi) takeover
(vii) horizontal
(viii) vertical
(ix) lateral
(x) backwards

9.2 (i) Technical economies of scale on production
(ii) Managerial economies where functions could be combined, for example accountancy
(iii) Trading economies such as bulk buying
(iv) Financial economies – should be able to borrow money at lower interest rates
(v) Research and Development economies could be achieved

9.3 (i) increasing bureaucracy and loss of control
(ii) poorer labour relations
(iii) difficulties of communication in a larger business

9.4 (i) *primary* – natural goods
(ii) *secondary* – produced goods
(iii) *tertiary* – services

9.5 (i) economies of scale
(ii) increase market share
(iii) fend off competition

9.6 (i) economies of scale
(ii) forward to get closer to market
(iii) backwards easier access to raw materials

9.7 (i) not solely reliant on one product or industry
(ii) functional duties can be shared, for example IT

9.8 *Advantages*

(i) workers better at job, so greater output
(ii) market dictates specialists, for example lawyers

Disadvantages

(i) job repetition
(ii) specialisation leads to functional divisions within the company

9.9 (i) economy
(ii) effectiveness
(iii) efficiency

9.10 (i) division of profits – dividends or managers' bonuses
(ii) time scale – managers appraised on short-term results
(iii) takeovers – higher share price vs redundancy
(iv) Annual general meeting (AGM) – re-elect the directors or not

? Multiple choice questions

9.1 If Tesco plc acquired a food processing company, this would be an example of

A horizontal integration
B vertical integration backwards
C vertical integration forwards
D conglomerate diversification

9.2 Which of the following is not a strategic argument for horizontal integration?

A to increase market share
B to pool technology
C to achieve economies of scale
D to reduce entry costs

9.3 Which one of the following will tend to increase competition within an industry?

A barriers to entry
B Government regulation
C horizontal integration
D low fixed costs

9.4 Which of the following are examples of internal economies?

(i) technical economies
(ii) financial economies
(iii) trading economies
(iv) managerial economies

A (i)
B (i) and (ii)
C (ii), (iii) and (iv)
D (i), (ii), (iii) and (iv)

9.5 The Monopolies and Mergers Commission/Competition Commission was set up

A to create more jobs
B to prevent regional inequality
C to see how public interest was affected where one firm or more controlled the market
D to improve industrial relations

Multiple choice solutions

9.1 **B**

If Tesco plc acquired a food processing company, this would be an example of vertical integration backwards.

9.2 **D**

By reducing entry costs, this allows more firms into the market which is not a strategic argument for horizontal integration.

9.3 **D**

Low fixed costs will encourage more firms to enter a market, thereby increasing competition within an industry.

9.4 **D**

Technical, financial, trading and managerial are all examples of internal economies of scale.

9.5 **C**

The Monopolies and Mergers Commission/Competition Commission was set up to see how public interest was affected where one firm or more controlled the market.

10 Market Structure

Market Structure 10

Concepts and definitions questions

10.1 Fill in the blanks

(i) A person running their own business is known as a ________ ________.
(ii) Two or more people running a business without limited liability are running a ________.
(iii) A business organisation regulated by The Companies Act and owned by shareholders with limited liability status is known as a _______ _______ ______.
(iv) A company which is allowed to sell shares to the public has the following initials at the end of its name ________.
(v) In a perfectly competitive market, all individual consumers and producers are said to be price ________.
(vi) In a perfectly competitive market, products are said to be ________.
(vii) The equilibrium of a firm operating under conditions of monopolistic competition where the average cost is still falling is operating at ________ ________.
(viii) The main difference between monopolistic competition and oligopoly is that in oligopolistic markets there are ________ ________ ________.
(ix) A monopolist has the ability to make ________ profits in the long run.
(x) The policy of pricing goods below their costs of production is known as ________ pricing.

10.2 Although the model of perfect competition is hypothetical, it contains three economic optimal positions. What are they and what is the significance of them?

(i)
(ii)
(iii)

10.3 A monopoly exists when one producer controls the whole market. This is because there are barriers preventing other firms from entering the industry. State six types of barriers that can exist.

(i)
(ii)
(iii)
(iv)
(v)
(vi)

10.4 Price discrimination occurs where a product or service is sold at different prices in different markets. For price discrimination to work, the three conditions necessary are

(i)
(ii)
(iii)

10.5 Consider the diagram below of a monopolist producer.

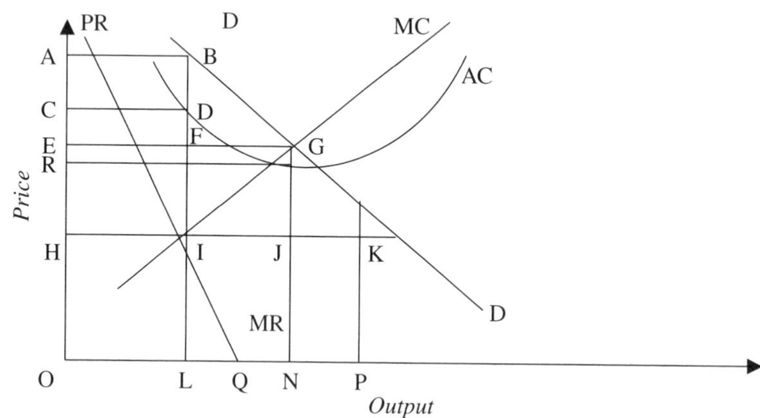

(i) What is the monopolist's profit maximising output?
(ii) What profit is made at this level of output?
(iii) What level of output would the monopolist produce at, if he was trying to maximise total revenue?
(iv) What level of output would the monopolist produce at, if he was trying to maximise market share?
(v) If this monopolist operated a policy of marginal cost pricing, what would be the increase in consumer surplus?
(vi) If this firm had to set price equal to the lowest average cost what price would be charged?

10.6 What is the most recent legislation designed to regulate monopolies and how does it differ from the Monopolies and Mergers Commission?

10.7 Explain, with an appropriate diagram, the kinked demand curve model of oligopoly.

10.8 Neoclassical theory suggests that all firms seek to maximise profits. In oligopolistic markets what other objectives might the firm have and why?

(i)
(ii)
(iii)
(iv)

10.9 What is a natural monopoly? Why might it be the case that a consumer might be better off in such a market?

10.10 Comparisons between perfect and imperfect markets.

	Perfect competition	*Monopolistic competition*	*Oligopoly*	*Monopoly*
No. of firms				
Type of products				
Price competition				
Type of demand curve				
Information				
Barriers to entry				
Exists in real life				

Complete each column for perfect competition, monopolistic competition, oligopoly and monopoly.

✓ Concepts and definitions solutions

10.1 (i) sole trader
(ii) partnership
(iii) private limited company
(iv) plc
(v) takers
(vi) homogeneous
(vii) excess capacity
(viii) barriers to entry
(ix) excess
(x) predatory

10.2 (i) marginal cost = marginal revenue
profits are maximised
(ii) average cost = marginal cost
average cost is minimised
(iii) marginal cost = price
society welfare is maximised

10.3 (i) control of supply – natural
(ii) advertising – artificial
(iii) high fixed costs – natural
(iv) patents – artificial
(v) regulation – artificial
(vi) Government licences, for example television – artificial

10.4 (i) control supply
(ii) identify at least two separate markets, that is, different elasticities of demand
(iii) prevent those who pay lower price from selling to those prepared to pay higher price

10.5 (i) OL, where MC = MR
(ii) ABCD
(iii) OQ, where MR = 0
(iv) where AC = demand
(v) BFG
(vi) OR

10.6 The most recent legislation designed to regulate monopolies in the United Kingdom is the Competition Act of 2000 which allows the Government to investigate companies who abuse their position of market power on a national or local basis and to investigate industries where restrictive practices take place.

10.7 Kinked demand curve

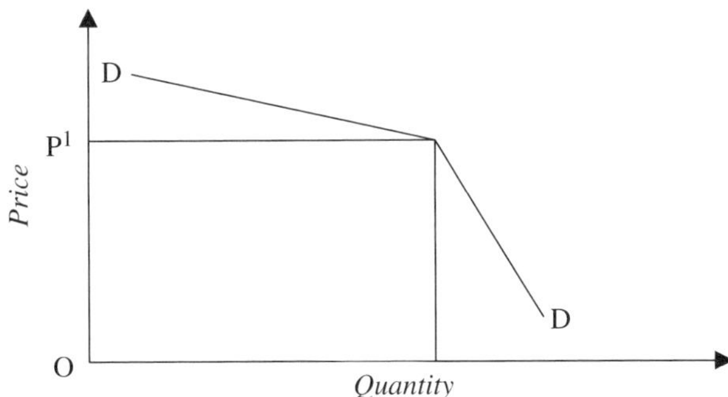

With kinked demand curve, producer is faced with worst-case scenario. An elastic demand curve above prevailing price and output, and inelastic demand below it.

10.8 (i) maximise market share – survival
(ii) maximise revenue – maximise managers' salaries
(iii) satisfices – keep all stakeholders happy
(iv) prevent new firms from entering the market. Spend money on advertising and branding.

10.9 A natural monopoly is one where cost per unit falls as output rises. A consumer might be better off because one firm could produce more cheaply and competition would lead to inefficiency.

10.10

	Perfect competition	*Monopolistic competition*	*Oligopoly*	*Monopoly*
No. of firms	many	many	few	one
Type of products	homogeneous	slightly differential	differential	one
Price competition	perfect	some	avoided	none
Type of demand curve	perfectly elastic	elastic	inelastic	inelastic
Information	perfect	perfect	imperfect	imperfect
Barriers to entry	none	none	many	impossible to enter
Exists in real life	no	becoming extinct	the norm	where govts. allow

? Multiple choice questions

10.1 Which one of the following would act as a barrier to entry to a new firm trying to enter a market?

A perfect knowledge
B consumer sovereignty
C branding
D low fixed costs of production

10.2 Which of the following is an artificial barrier to entry?

A economies of scale
B high fixed costs of production
C Government issue of patents
D price fixing

10.3 A monopsony is

A a market with one buyer
B a market with one seller
C a market with few buyers
D a market with few sellers

10.4 Which of the following is not a condition of monopolistic competition?

A many buyers and sellers
B excess capacity
C marginal revenue below average revenue
D infinitely inelastic demand curve

10.5 Which of the following are examples of price discrimination?

(i) first and second-class rail fares
(ii) business and economy class flights
(iii) peak and off-peak rail fares
(iv) a doctor charging wealthier clients higher consultancy fees

A (i) and (ii)
B (ii) and (iii)
C (ii) and (iv)
D (iii) and (iv)

10.6 The model of monopolistic competition has been criticised because of excess capacity. This implies that

A firms do not maximise profits
B excess profits are made
C firms produce at an output below their optimum capacity
D there are barriers to entry

10.7 A natural monopoly may be beneficial to the consumer because

A the company controls a larger share of the market
B the company can obtain economies of scale
C the company can restrict output
D none of the above

10.8 Which of the following is incompatible with perfect competition?

A marginal cost = marginal revenue
B marginal cost = average cost
C marginal cost = price
D marginal revenue = below average revenue

10.9 The kinked demand curve in oligopoly can be explained by

A monopoly power enjoyed by oligopolists
B other firms will follow a price rise but not a reduction
C other firms will follow a price reduction but not a price rise
D firms will form a cartel to fix price

10.10 All of the following are examples of anti-competitive behaviour by large firms except

A cartels
B price fixing with retailers
C offering retailers higher discounts if they do not stock competitors' products
D extensive advertising

✓ Multiple choice solutions

10.1 **C**

Branding is the only barrier to entry of the alternatives offered.

10.2 **C**

An artificial barrier is one created by government – an example being the issue of patents.

10.3 **A**

A monopsony is a market with one buyer.

10.4 **D**

An infinitely inelastic demand curve is not a condition of monopolistic competition.

10.5 **D**

Alternatives (iii) and (iv) are examples of price discrimination because the products or services are the same, alternatives (i) and (ii) are selling different products and services.

10.6 **C**

Excess capacity implies that firms produce at an output below their optimum capacity.

10.7 **B**

A natural monopoly may be beneficial to the consumer because the company can obtain economies of scale.

10.8 **D**

Marginal revenue = below average revenue is not compatible with perfect competition.

10.9 **C**

The kinked demand curve in oligopoly can be explained by other firms following a price reduction but not a price rise.

10.10 **D**

Extensive advertising is not an example of anti-competitive behaviour by large firms.

The Public Sector and Regulation

The Public Sector and Regulation 11

? Concepts and definitions questions

11.1 State six arguments in favour of nationalisation.

(i)
(ii)
(iii)
(iv)
(v)
(vi)

11.2 State five arguments in favour of privatisation.

(i)
(ii)
(iii)
(iv)
(v)

11.3 State six criticisms of privatisation.

(i)
(ii)
(iii)
(iv)
(v)
(vi)

11.4 What is the difference between a public good and a merit good?

11.5 Why do governments establish official bodies to regulate privatised utilities?

11.6 State five pieces of legislation involving government regulation of industry.

(i)
(ii)
(iii)
(iv)
(v)

11.7 What is a contestable market?

✓ Concepts and definitions solutions

11.1 Arguments in favour of nationalisation

(i) natural monopolies such as public utilities
(ii) sufficient capital available for investment because of government support
(iii) provision of uneconomical services, for example rural transport
(iv) strategic control over key industries
(v) protects employment, for example keeping open uneconomic coal mines
(vi) leads to a more even and fairer distribution of income and wealth.

11.2 Arguments in favour of privatisation

(i) improved efficiency: many state industries were overmanned
(ii) privatisation has led to wider share ownership which gives workers better understanding of the profit motive
(iii) competition should lead to better quality and lower prices
(iv) profits made by privatised firms will provide extra funding to the treasury
(v) privatisation should lead to greater economic freedom.

11.3 Six criticisms of privatisation

(i) Many government assets were sold off below their market price. Harold MacMillan described this as "selling off the family silver".
(ii) Executives have paid themselves excessive salaries in protected markets.
(iii) Public sector monopolies have just been transferred to private sector monopolies.
(iv) Many shares were sold to overseas individuals and institutions, thereby weakening The Balance of Payments.
(v) Fewer services and higher prices, for example rural transport.
(vi) Loss of jobs: in 1993 British Telecom shed 15,000 jobs.

11.4 Public goods are products, such as defence where the consumption by one person does not diminish someone else's (non-rivalry) and that person cannot stop someone else benefiting from it (non-exclusivity).

A merit good is one which left purely to market forces would lead to an underprovision of that good or service, for example education. A merit good is often free to the consumer but it is not a free good, for example primary school education.

11.5 Many industries in the United Kingdom were privatised and regulated. With public monopolies being transferred to private monopolies, the government accepted the need to create regulatory watchdogs. The role of specific industry regulators (SIRS) is twofold.

(i) SIRS can introduce an element of competition by setting price caps and performance standards.
(ii) SIRS can speed up the introduction of competition in such markets by reducing barriers to entry.

11.6 (i) Restrictive Practices Act 1956
(ii) Competition Act 1980
(iii) Companies Act 1989
(iv) Competition Act 2000
(v) Enterprise Act 2003.

11.7 In some markets, there are few firms but entry and exit is so easy that competition from potential new firms is strong. A market in which potential entry is free is called a contestable market. An example would be a local private bus route. Firms could easily switch their buses from one route to another with virtually no entry or exit costs.

? Multiple choice questions

11.1 A pure public good is one which

A no individual can be excluded from consuming it
B when consumed by one person implies less consumption by others
C involves no social costs in production
D is produced by the state

11.2 A chemical company has reduced the level of pollution from its factory. This will lead to a fall in

A social costs
B social benefits
C average costs
D marginal costs

11.3 Which of the following are examples of merit goods?

(i) defence
(ii) health
(iii) education
(iv) water

A (i) and (ii)
B (i) and (iii)
C (ii) and (iii)
D (ii) and (iv)

11.4 A contestable market is one where

A firms bid against each other to get a contract
B entry and exit are relatively easy
C the utilities are regulated
D firms cannot predict demand

11.5 A good which is characterised by both rivalry and excludability is known as

A a merit good
B a public good
C a private good
D none of the above

11.6 Which of the following is not an argument in favour of privatisation?

A a reduction in bureaucracy
B a more even distribution of income and wealth
C increased competition between firms in the same industry
D greater consumer choice

11.7 Which one of the following is not a valid economic reason for producing goods and services by the state?

A it is a merit good
B it is a public good
C it is a natural monopoly
D it is a necessity which is consumed by everyone

11.8 When privatisation took place in the United Kingdom

A assets were transferred from the public sector and money went to the government
B assets were transferred from the private sector and money went to the government
C assets were transferred from the private sector and money went to the private sector
D assets were transferred from the public sector and money went to the private sector

11.9 The production of a good results in a positive externality. The government should

A give the producer a subsidy which reflects the marginal benefit from the consumption of the good
B give the producer a subsidy which reflects the marginal cost of the externality
C impose a tax on the producer which reflects the marginal benefit derived from consumption
D impose a tax on the producer which reflects the marginal cost of the externality

11.10 The government may discourage horizontal mergers in manufacturing industry because

A by controlling the sources of supply, the merged firms will have unfair advantages over its rivals
B the merged firms will be unable to secure economies of scale
C consumers may lose out if the merged firm acquires market dominance
D there is a lack of synergy between the two companies

Multiple choice solutions

11.1 **A**

A pure public good is one which no individual can be excluded from consuming it.

11.2 **A**

If a chemical company has reduced the level of pollution from its factory, this will lead to a fall in social costs.

11.3 **C**

Health and education are examples of merit goods. Defence is a public good and water is a necessity.

11.4 **B**

A contestable market is one where entry and exit are relatively easy.

11.5 **C**

A good which is characterised by both rivalry and excludability is known as a private good.

11.6 **B**

Privatisation will lead to a less even distribution of income and wealth.

11.7 **D**

Bread is a necessity consumed by everyone but it is not produced by the state.

11.8 **A**

When privatisation took place in the United Kingdom, assets were transferred from the public sector and money went to the government.

11.9 **A**

If the production of a good results in a positive externality, the government should give the producer a subsidy which reflects the marginal benefit from the consumption of the good.

11.10 **C**

The government may discourage horizontal mergers in manufacturing industry because consumers may lose out if the merged firm acquires market dominance.

The Financial System

The Financial System

The Financial System

12

Concepts and definitions questions

12.1 According to Keynes, there are three reasons why we hold money. They are

(i)
(ii)
(iii)

12.2 The factors which influence our demand for holding money are

(i)
(ii)
(iii)

12.3 *Bond prices and interest rates*

The current market rate of interest is 10%. The government is issuing new bonds at £100 each offering a yield of 10%.

(i) What would be the maximum price you would pay for the bond?
(ii) If market rates of interest rose and the yield on the bond remained at 10% what would happen to the price of the bond?
(iii) If market rates fall and the bond remained at 10% what would happen to the price of the bond?
(iv) If interest rates were 5% what would be the maximum price you pay for the bond?
(v) If interest rates were 20% what would be the maximum price you would pay?
(vi) How much would the government redeem the bond for?

12.4 *Liquidity preference theory*

(i) If the money supply is originally at MS1 what is the rate of interest?
(ii) What is the purpose of shifting money supply from MS1 to MS2?
(iii) How does the Bank of England manage to shift money supply from MS1 to MS2?
(iv) The schedule is known as the _________ _________ _________.

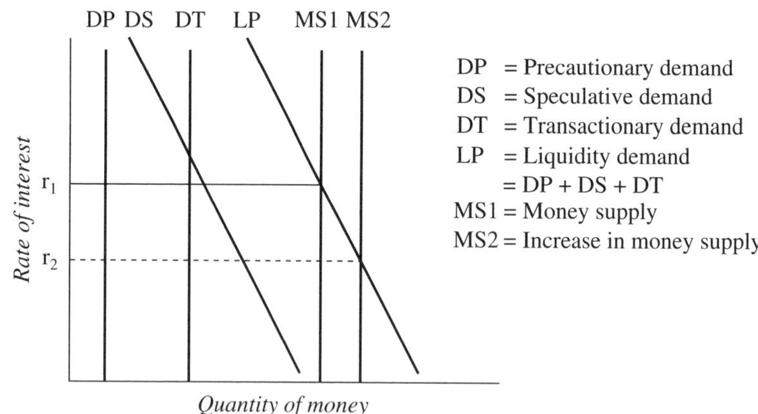

12.5 What factors would affect the rates of interest charged on a specific loan?

(i)
(ii)
(iii)
(iv)
(v)

12.6 The following financial data refer to an economy over a five-year period:

Interest rates	*2000*	*2001*	*2002*	*2003*	*2004*
Base rate	8.5	7.0	5.5	6.8	5.8
Instant access deposit rate	6.3	4.9	3.8	4.2	2.8
90-day access deposit	8.8	6.2	4.5	4.9	3.9
Mortgage rate	11.0	9.4	7.7	8.4	7.0

(i) What is the base rate?
(ii) What is instant access deposit rate?
(iii) What is 90-day access deposit rate?
(iv) What is mortgage rate?
(v) Why is instant access rate below 90-day access rate?
(vi) Why is mortgage rate higher than base rates?
(vii) What is the difference between nominal and real rates of interest?
(viii) If the retail price index for 2000 shows a rate of inflation of 4%, what was the real rate of interest in that year?

12.7 There are three ways for the government to control the money supply:

(i) Interest rates
(ii) Open market operations
(iii) Reserve asset ratios

If monetary policy were to be relaxed, which combination of policies would be appropriate?

A Interest rates to be raised/cut
B The government to buy/sell government securities
C The reserve asset ratio to be reduced/increased

12.8 *Yield curve*

The yield curve represents the term "structure of interest rates" which is concerned with the way the yield of a security varies according to the duration of the security. It normally slopes upwards. This can be explained in terms of

(i)
(ii)
(iii)

12.9 The following statements are either true or false

(i) Precautionary demand for money is determined by interest rates.
(ii) The price of a bond is inversely related to market rates of interest.
(iii) According to the liquidity preference theory, the transactions demand for money is completely interest inelastic.
(iv) Narrow money is more liquid than broad money.
(v) The loanable funds theory is the monetarist view of how interest rates work.
(vi) Short-term interest rates tend to be higher than long-term interest rates.
(vii) Banks will lend money to their good customers at base rates.
(viii) A yield curve which rises from left to right indicates that interest rates are expected to rise in the future.
(ix) The nominal rate of interest is always above the real rate of interest.
(x) The higher the risks, the higher the rate of interest.

12.10 The major function of money is its function as a medium of exchange. What must money possess in order for this function to work.

Concepts and definitions solutions

12.1 (i) transactions demand
(ii) precautionary demand
(iii) speculative demand

12.2 (i) income
(ii) nature of the individual
(iii) interest rates

12.3 (i) £100 because I would get the same yield by putting the money in a bank account.
(ii) Fall because the bond now becomes a less attractive investment in relation to others.
(iii) Rise because the bond now becomes a more attractive investment in relation to others.
(iv) It is a question of equalising the yields so if interest rates are 5%, this would give us a 5% yield on a bond if we paid £200 for it.
(v) As in (iv) we would get a yield of 20% if we paid £50 for the bond. If we bought 2 for £100 this would give us a yield of £20 or 20%.
(vi) Always at face value £100.

12.4 (i) R1
(ii) to reduce interest rates
(iii) open market operations – buying bonds therefore increasing bank liquidity
(iv) liquidity preference schedule

12.5 (i) length of the loan
(ii) risk of the loan
(iii) size of the loan
(iv) rate of return required by lender
(v) level of competition in the money market

12.6 (i) Base rate is the standard rate from which all bank lending rates are set.
(ii) It is the rate a bank will pay someone, holding a deposit account, who wants to be able to withdraw money at any time.
(iii) It is the rate a bank will pay someone, holding a deposit account, who must wait for 3 months before they can withdraw any money from that account.
(iv) The mortgage rate is the rate at which building societies will lend money to individuals who wish to borrow money to purchase property.
(v) With 90-day access, lenders have access to your funds for an extra 90 days which they can invest at a higher rate.
(vi) Base rate is never the rate at which banks lend, for personal overdrafts they normally charge about 5% above the base rate which is higher than the mortgage rate.
(vii) The rate of inflation.
(viii) 4.5%.

12.7 A cut
B buy
C reduced

12.8 (i) *Expectations theory*: Investors expect interest rates to rise in the future.
(ii) *Liquidity preference theory*: Investors have a natural preference for holding cash, therefore must be compensated for being deprived of their cash.
(iii) *Market segment theory*: There are different types of investors who are interested in different segments of the curve, for example banks will invest at the short end while pension funds will invest at the longer end of the scale.

12.9 (i) False
(ii) True
(iii) True
(iv) True
(v) True
(vi) False
(vii) False
(viii) True
(ix) False
(x) True

12.10 (i) it must be widely acceptable
(ii) it must have a high value weight ratio
(iii) it must be divisible to settle debts of different denominations
(iv) it must not be easily produced, counterfeited or debased in value

? Multiple choice questions

12.1 The liquidity preference schedule states that

A people prefer to hold money rather than other forms of wealth when the rate of return is equal
B people prefer to hold money when the rate of interest is high
C banks prefer lending short-term to their customers
D people prefer to hold bonds and equities

12.2 Speculative demand for money is a function of

A income
B wealth
C interest rates
D the nature of the individual

12.3 If the central bank pursues an expansionary open market operations policy, it will

A sell securities on the open market
B buy securities from non-government holders
C increase the reverse asset ratio
D decrease the reserve asset ratio

12.4 If a bank buys a bill of exchange worth £100 in 3 months time for £96, the discount rate would be approximately

A 4%
B 16%
C 20%
D 24%

12.5 Which of the following is never an asset of a clearing bank?

A cash
B loans made to a company
C a customer's deposit account
D balances held with the Bank of England

12.6 In the Keynesian theory of demand for money, the transactions demand for money is determined by

A the rate of interest
B the level of consumers' income
C expected changes in equity prices
D the amount of money in circulation

12.7 According to the classical view of interest rates, the supply of loanable funds will be

A negatively related to interest rates
B positively related to interest rates
C unrelated to interest rates
D linked to the demand for money

12.8 The crowding out effect is caused by

A a rise in interest rates reducing private sector investment
B a rise in interest rates reducing public sector investment
C a fall in interest rates reducing savings
D a rise in interest rates raising mortgage rates

12.9 If the reserve asset ratio was 25%, how much money could a bank create from an initial deposit of £100?

A £100
B £200
C £300
D £400

12.10 If the market rate of interest falls, the price of bonds will

A rise
B fall
C stay the same
D could go up or down

Multiple choice solutions

12.1 **A**

The liquidity preference schedule states that people prefer to hold money rather than other forms of wealth when the rate of return is equal.

12.2 **C**

Transactions demand is a function of income and wealth.
Precautionary demand is down to the individual.
Speculative demand is a function of different interest rates.

12.3 **B**

If the central bank pursues an expansionary open market operations policy it will buy securities from the public who will in turn hold the money with the banking sector, thus increasing the liquidity of the banking sector.

12.4 **B**

The bank is making a rate of return of just over 4% over a period of 3 months but interest rates are based on an annual figure giving a return of just over 16%.

12.5 **C**

A customer's deposit account is an asset of the customer so is a liability to a clearing bank.

12.6 **B**

Transactions demand is determined by consumers' income.

12.7 **B**

According to the classical view of interest rates, the supply of loanable funds will be positively related to interest rates.

12.8 **A**

The crowding out effect is caused by a rise in interest rates as the public sector competes with the private sector for funds, thus reducing private sector investment.

12.9 **D**

Credit multiplier = 1/RAR = 1/25% = 4   4 × £100 = £400

12.10 **A**

If the market rate of interest falls, the price of bonds will rise because they become a more attractive investment in relation to others.

Financial Markets

Financial Markets 13

Concepts and definitions questions

13.1 The stock exchange has two roles. First, to raise new finance for companies and governments, and secondly, to provide a secondary market for investors. Who are the key institutional investors?

(i)
(ii)
(iii)
(iv)
(v)

13.2 The stock exchange runs four types of markets. They are

(i)
(ii)
(iii)
(iv)

13.3 What do the following initials stand for?

(i) FTSE
(ii) GEMM
(iii) SEAQ
(iv) TOPIC
(v) CREST
(vi) SEDOL
(vii) AIM
(viii) USM
(ix) LIBID
(x) LIBOR

13.4 Merchant banks, now referred to as Investment banks, offer the following services to customers:

(i)
(ii)
(iii)
(iv)
(v)
(vi)

13.5 In recent years the role of building societies is similar to that of banks, although three major differences still prevail. They are

(i)
(ii)
(iii)

13.6 State five characteristics of an investment trust.

(i)
(ii)
(iii)
(iv)
(v)

13.7 A unit trust performs a similar role to an investment trust but they are different. Three differences are:

(i)
(ii)
(iii)

13.8 *Venture capital*

The venture capital market exists to promote the growth of small businesses. This type of finance is equity rather than debt where the venture capitalists actually take a share in the business. The main providers of venture capital are

(i)
(ii)
(iii)
(iv)
(v)

13.9 There are several types of long-term capital. They include

(i)
(ii)
(iii)
(iv)
(v)

13.10 (i) The most frequently quoted measure of the US stock market is the ________ ________ Index.
(ii) The main share index in Japan is known as the ________ Index.
(iii) The money market used by the government when it requires short-term funds is the ________ market.
(iv) A market in sterling in which banks borrow and lend between themselves is known as the ________ ________ market.
(v) A deposit with a bank in a currency other than that of the country in which the bank is located is called the ________ ________ market.
(vi) Debt securities issued by listed companies is known as the ________ ________ market.
(vii) The markets in (iv), (v) and (vi) are all examples of ________ markets.

(viii) An unconditional promise to pay a certain amount of money at a given time in the future is a ________ ________ ________.

(ix) A bill of exchange with no supplier guaranteed by a bank is called a ________ ________.

(x) A bill of exchange that has been accepted by an eligible bank or clearing house is known as an ________ ________.

✓ Concepts and definitions solutions

13.1
(i) Pension funds
(ii) Insurance companies
(iii) Unit trusts
(iv) Investment trusts
(v) Fund managers

13.2
(i) Gilt-edged
(ii) UK fully listed securities
(iii) Alternative Investment Market (AIM)
(iv) Overseas securities

13.3
(i) Financial Times Stock Exchange Index
(ii) Gilt-Edged Market Markers
(iii) Stock Exchange Automated Quotation System
(iv) A computerised system giving access to different information systems, for example SEAQ
(v) The computer system which records the holdings of securities and the settlements of traders
(vi) Stock Exchange Daily Official List
(vii) Alternative Investment Market
(viii) Unlisted Securities Market
(ix) London Inter Bank Bid Rate
(x) London Inter Bank Offer Rate

13.4
(i) advice on takeover and mergers
(ii) advice on raising capital
(iii) act as an issuing house
(iv) underwrites new issues
(v) issue Eurobonds
(vi) provide fund management

13.5
(i) The building societies are still prevalent in house purchase mortgages.
(ii) The building society deposits and loans tend to be for smaller amounts.
(iii) The building societies still tend to lend long-term and not get involved in the money market.

13.6
(i) They are a company.
(ii) They are listed on the stock exchange.
(iii) They have equity and debt capital.
(iv) They invest in the shares of other companies.
(v) They provide an opportunity for small investors to diversify their investment.

13.7
(i) They are a trust in the legal sense.
(ii) Money raised comes only from investors.
(iii) The Securities and Investment Board only allow unit trusts to undertake in certain investments.

13.8
(i) Investment Trusts
(ii) Merchant Banks
(iii) Local authorities
(iv) Regional Enterprise Boards
(v) Industrial and Commercial Finance Corporation

13.9
(i) Ordinary shares
(ii) Preference shares
(iii) Debentures
(iv) Convertible stocks
(v) Derivatives

13.10
(i) Dow Jones
(ii) Nikkei
(iii) Discount
(iv) Sterling interbank
(v) Eurocurrency
(vi) Commercial paper
(vii) Parallel
(viii) Bill of exchange
(ix) Bankers' acceptance
(x) Eligible bill

? Multiple choice questions

13.1 Which of the following does not engage in the buying and selling of shares in other companies?

A Unit trusts
B Investment trusts
C Pension funds
D The Stock Exchange

13.2 Which of the following institutions does not invest in the capital markets?

A Pension funds
B Unit trusts
C Insurance companies
D Discount houses

13.3 Equity finance in high-risk enterprises is known as

A Venture capital
B Working capital
C Debentures
D A bill of exchange

13.4 In the international capital markets, long-term capital would be supplied by the

A Eurobond market
B Eurocredit market
C Eurocurrency market
D The stock market

13.5 In the alternative investment market, firms can raise funds up to

A £50,000
B £250,000
C £750,000
D £1,000,000

13.6 Which of the following is one of the major differences between an investment trust and a unit trust?

A An investment trust provides an opportunity for small investors to diversify their investment
B A unit trust invests in the shares of other companies
C A unit trust has no debt finance
D An investment trust is listed on the stock exchange

13.7 Which of the following is not a source of long-term capital?

A Debentures
B Preference shares
C Factoring
D Convertible stocks

13.8 An investor who buys a call option is

A Selling the right to buy shares at a particular price
B Selling the right to sell shares at a particular price

C Buying the right to buy shares at a particular price
D Buying the right to sell shares at a particular price

13.9 A broker will buy shares from an investor. This is known as the

A Bid price
B Spread price
C Transaction price
D Offer price

13.10 If a merchant bank underwrites a new £100 million £1 share issue and the market purchases 90 million shares at 90p per share, how much would the merchant bank have to make up to the company?

A nothing
B £9 million
C £10 million
D £19 million

Multiple choice solutions

13.1 **D**

You can buy and sell shares through the Stock Exchange but they do not actually engage in the market themselves.

13.2 **D**

This question is testing candidates ability to distinguish between short-term money markets and long-term capital markets.
Capital markets – A, B and C
Money market – Discount houses.

13.3 **A**

People or institutions who put their money into high-risk equity finance projects are known as venture capitalists.

13.4 **A**

Eurocredit and Eurocurrency are short-term capital markets.
The Stock Exchange is primarily domestic capital.

13.5 **B**

Firms can raise money up to £250,000.

13.6 **C**

An investment trust and a unit trust are quite similar like statements A, B and D but a unit trust is financed by investors' money alone.

13.7 **C**

Debentures, preference shares and convertible stocks are all examples of long-term capital. Factoring is where a company sells part or all of its debtors to a third party. This is regarded as working capital.

13.8 **C**

An investor who buys a call option is buying the right to buy shares at a particular price. Buying the right to sell at a particular price is a put option.

13.9 **A**

Bid price is the price at which the broker will buy shares from an investor.

13.10 **D**

If the bank underwrites the issue to the tune of £100 million and the public only buy 90 million shares at 90p then only £81 million is raised on the issue. The bank would, therefore, have to make up the difference, that is, £19 million.

14 Monetary Policy

Monetary Policy 14

Concepts and definitions questions

14.1 The quantity theory of money states that MV = PT, that is, the supply of money = the demand for money, where

(i) M is
(ii) V is
(iii) P is
(iv) T is

14.2 What are the three main methods by which the Bank of England seek to control the money supply?

(i)
(ii)
(iii)

14.3 If the central bank were to increase interest rates, what would be the economic consequences?

(i)
(ii)
(iii)
(iv)
(v)

14.4 What was the theoretical basis for medium-term financial strategy?

14.5 What would be the value of the credit multiplier if the reserve asset ratio was

(i) 10%
(ii) 20%
(iii) 25%
(iv) 40%
(v) 50%

14.6 The figures below represent a simplified balance sheet of a clearing bank (A)

Assets		*Liabilities*	
Loans	£80m	Deposits	£100m
Cash	£20m		
	£100m		£100m

The government decides to sell some government securities of which £5 million worth are purchased by customers of Bank A.

(i) Reconstruct the balance sheet to show the impact of these purchases.
(ii) Reconstruct the balance sheet to show that a reserve asset ratio of 20% has been maintained.

14.7 What is inflation targeting?

14.8 How might the effects of a change in the money supply differ between the short and the long run?

14.9 Explain the difference between the Keynesian and monetarist views of the following economic variables.

(i) Demand for money
(ii) Supply of money
(iii) Interest rates
(iv) Investment
(v) Savings
(vi) Government policy

14.10 What are the advantages of having an independent central bank?

(i)
(ii)

✓ Concepts and definitions solutions

14.1 (i) M = money supply
(ii) V = velocity of circulation
(iii) P = price level
(iv) T = transactions demand

14.2 (i) *Interest rates*: Affect the price at which individuals and institutions can borrow money.
(ii) *Open market operations*: The buying and selling of government securities.
(iii) *Reserve asset ratio*: The proportion of assets banks must hold in liquid format.

14.3 (i) Consumer expenditure would fall
(ii) The market price of assets would fall
(iii) Foreign funds would be attracted to UK financial institutions
(iv) The exchange rate would rise
(v) Inflation should fall

14.4 The theoretical basis for the Medium-Term Financial Strategy (MTFS) was that excessive public spending led to budget deficits which in turn raised monetary growth and fuelled demand-pull inflation when supply did not keep pace with this growth.

14.5 The credit multiplier is found by taking the reciprocal of the reserve asset ratio so

(i) 1/(1/10) = 10
(ii) 1/(1/5) = 5
(iii) 1/(1/4) = 4
(iv) 1/(4/10) = 2.5
(v) 1/(1/2) = 2

14.6 (i)

Assets		*Liabilities*	
Loans	£80m	Deposits	£95m
Cash	£15m		
	£95m		£95m

(ii)

Assets		*Liabilities*	
Loans	£76m	Deposits	£95m
Cash	£19m		
	£95m		£95m

14.7 Inflation targeting has been in existence since 1997 when the Bank of England was given independence in monetary policy and was given an inflation target of 2.5% by the Chancellor.

14.8 In the short run an increase in the money supply will increase real output, in the long run it will only increase prices.

14.9

	Economic variable	*Keynesians*	*Monetarists*
(i)	Demand for money	Expressed by the liquidity preference schedules, savings may be held in the form of cash ("idle balances") if interest rates are low and speculators believe that they will rise	Money mainly demanded for transactions. Any portion of income not spent will be saved in an interest-bearing form. Idle balances will not be held
(ii)	Supply (stock) of money	Interacts with the speculative demand for money to set interest rates. Additional money entering the system will be accompanied by lower interest rates which will induce spectators to exchange some of their bonds for cash	The quantity theory of money predicts that the money supply is closely connected with the rate of inflation. Additional money entering the system will be spent (as people do not hold idle balances), causing prices to rise
(iii)	Interest rates	Set by the interaction of the demand for, and supply of, money	Set by the interaction of the demand for, and supply of, loanable funds investment and savings
(iv)	Investment	Influenced by interest rates (compared to the marginal efficiency of capital), but much more strongly by entrepreneurs' animal spirits	Determined primarily by interest rates
(v)	Savings	Determined by the level of income, as the residual after the consumption decision is made (using the consumption function)	Determined primarily by interest rates
(vi)	Government policy	Control the economy using demand management	Allow market forces to govern. Ensure that markets are as competitive as possible and, by supply growth, prevent inflation from distorting price signals

14.10 (i) Free from political interference
(ii) Can concentrate on inflation

Multiple choice questions

14.1 Which of the following would be likely to occur if there was a reduction in the money supply in an economy?

(i) a fall in the rate of inflation
(ii) a rise in the exchange rate
(iii) a rise in interest rate
(iv) an increase in the demand for money

A (i), (ii) and (iii) only
B (i), (ii) and (iv) only
C (i), (iii) and (iv) only
D (ii), (iii) and (iv) only

14.2 If the money supply is £25 million, and there are 500,000 spending transactions carried out on a weekly basis at an average price of £100 then the weekly velocity of circulation is

A 1
B 2
C 3
D 4

14.3 If the government were to pursue a contractionary monetary policy they would

A raise interest rates and sell securities
B lower interest rates and sell securities
C raise interest rates and buy securities
D lower interest rates and buy securities

14.4 Which of the following are not arguments in favour of an independent bank?

(i) not influenced by politics
(ii) concentrating on maintaining price stability
(iii) maintains fixed exchange rates
(iv) maintains floating exchange rates

A (i) and (ii)
B (ii) and (iii)
C (i) and (iv)
D (iii) and (iv)

14.5 Over the past few years, interest rates in the UK have been maintained at low levels. The major side effect of this policy is

A an increasing savings ratio
B a reduction in investment
C a housing boom
D a rise in stock market prices

14.6 The major impact of an increase in the reserve asset ratio would be

A to push up interest rates
B to reduce interest rates
C to reduce the level of liquidity in the banking sector
D to raise the level of liquidity in the banking sector

14.7 Which of the following is not a function of money?

A a store of value
B a medium of exchange
C a measure of value
D a hedge against inflation

14.8 If the Bank of England imposes a restriction on lending to property developers, this is an example of

A supply-side economics
B special directives
C open market operations
D Keynesian economics

14.9 When the Bank of England raises the intervention rate, which financial institutions feels the first impact?

A unit trusts
B finance houses
C investment trusts
D the discount markets

14.10 A 3 year gilt has a redemption yield of 6% and a 20 year gilt has a redemption yield of 5%. This would suggest

A interest rates are expected to rise
B a normal yield exists
C an inverse yield exists
D long term interest rates are higher than short term rates

✓ Multiple choice solutions

14.1 **A**

A reduction in the money supply would lead to a fall in the rate of inflation, a rise in the exchange rate and a rise in interest rates.

14.2 **B**

MV = PT
£25 million × V = 100 × 500,000 = £50 million
£25 million × 2 = £50 million so V = 2

14.3 **A**

If the government were to pursue a contractionary monetary policy they would raise interest rates so we can eliminate alternatives B and D.

They would sell securities which would be bought by cheques from the banking sector, thereby eliminating banking liquidity.

14.4 **D**

Alternatives (i) and (ii) are arguments in favour of a central bank.
Alternatives (iii) and (iv) have nothing to do with bank independence, therefore are not arguments in favour.

14.5 **C**

Sustained low interest rates have created a housing boom.

14.6 **C**

An increase in the reserve asset ratio would reduce the level of liquidity in the banking sector.

14.7 **D**

Money is all of the following except a hedge against inflation.

14.8 **B**

If the Bank of England imposes a restriction on lending to property developers, this is an example of special directives.

14.9 **D**

When the Bank of England raises the intervention rate the financial institutions which feel the first impact are the discount markets since they are involved in the short-term money market.

14.10 **C**

A falling or inverse yield curve implies that interest rates are expected to fall which is why 20 year rate is below 3 year rate.

The Macroeconomic Content of Business: The Domestic Economy

15

National Income

National Income 15

Concepts and definitions questions

15.1 What are the three methods by which national income statistics can be calculated?

(i)
(ii)
(iii)

15.2 Why do countries bother to calculate national income statistics?

(i)
(ii)
(iii)

15.3 Consider the following data

	Market prices £bn
Consumers' expenditure	115
General government final consumption	38
Gross domestic fixed capital formation	34
Value of increase in stocks and WIP	3
Exports	55
Imports	54
Net property income from abroad	1
Taxes	30
Subsidies	4
Capital consumption	22

(i) Calculate gross domestic product at market prices
(ii) Calculate gross national product at market prices
(iii) Calculate net national product at market prices
(iv) Calculate net national product at factor cost

15.4 The following figures are taken from the national accounts of a fictional country.

Income method

Income from employment and self-employment	110,000
Gross rental income	10,000
Gross trading profit of private companies	15,000
Gross trading surplus of public companies	2,000
less stock appreciation	6,000
Residual adjustment	2,000
Net property income from abroad	1,000
less depreciation	4,000

Expenditure method

Consumer expenditure	66,000
Government final expenditure	35,000
Gross domestic fixed capital formation	15,000
Value of physical increase in stocks	15,000
Net exports	10,000
less indirect taxes net of subsidies	8,000

(i) Show that the two methods give the same figure for gross domestic product at factor cost.
(ii) Find the value of gross domestic product at market prices.
(iii) Find the value of gross national product at factor cost.
(iv) Find the value of net national product at factor cost.
(v) Explain the need for the stock appreciation adjustment.
(vi) Explain why the value of physical increase in stocks appears in the expenditure method.
(vii) What do you think the residual adjustment represents?

15.5 The following questions relate to problems associated with measuring national income statistics.

(i) The existence of the black economy tends to over/under estimate national income statistics.
(ii) Services which are provided free of charge tend to over/under estimate national income statistics.
(iii) Producers who consume part of their output tend to over/under estimate national income statistics.
(iv) Government subsidies tend to over/under estimate national income statistics.
(v) Government taxation tends to over/under estimate national income statistics.

✓ Concepts and definitions solutions

15.1 (i) income
(ii) output
(iii) expenditure

15.2 (i) economic planning
(ii) to see if economy is rising or falling
(iii) to compare its growth rates with other countries

15.3 (i) £190bn (115 + 38 + 34 + 3 + 55 − 54)
(ii) £192bn (191 + 1)
(iii) £170bn (192 − 22)
(iv) £144bn (170 − 30 + 4)

15.4 (i) *Income method*

110,000 + 10,000 + 15,000 + 2,000 − 6,000 + 2,000 = 133,000

Expenditure method

66,000 + 35,000 + 15,000 + 15,000 + 10,000 − 8,000 = 133,000

(ii) 133,000 + 8,000 = 141,000
(iii) 133,000 + 1,000 = 134,000
(iv) 134,000 − 4,000 = 130,000
(v) Stock appreciation needs to be adjusted from income method since we are trying to measure what has been produced. A rise in the price of an asset, for example a house might make someone better off but there is no corresponding output.
(vi) Conversely, the value of physical increase in stocks represents output which has been produced but there is no corresponding expenditure.
(vii) By definition output = income = expenditure. However, with all statistics of this magnitude, errors and omissions take place.

15.5 (i) under
(ii) under
(iii) under
(iv) under
(v) over

Multiple choice questions

Questions 1–4 are based on the following data

	Market prices £m
Consumer expenditure	120
General government final consumption	30
Gross domestic fixed capital	35
Value of physical increase in stock	5
Exports	20
Imports	25
Net property income from abroad	1
Taxes	50
Subsidies	10
Capital consumption	25

15.1 GDP at market prices is

A £165m
B £185m
C £190m
D £210m

15.2 GNP at market prices is

A £165m
B £186m
C £190m
D £210m

15.3 GNP at factor cost is

A £146m
B £185m
C £186m
D £200m

15.4 Net national product at factor cost is

A £121m
B £146m
C £171m
D £186m

15.5 The following data relates to the national income of a given economy

	2005	*2006*
National income	520	625

Between 2005 and 2006 the retail price index rose from 100 to 110. After deflating the 2006 national income figures, the value of the national income for 2006 was

A 520
B 544
C 568
D 582

15.6 Which of the following would underestimate the real value of goods and services?

(i) the existence of the hidden economy
(ii) voluntary labour
(iii) inflation
(iv) capital consumption

A (i) and (ii)
B (ii) and (iii)
C (iii) and (iv)
D (ii) only

15.7 Which one of the following is not a transfer payment?

A pension
B student grant
C family allowance
D teacher's salary

15.8 In which method of measuring national income statistics might you encounter double counting?

A expenditure and income
B expenditure and output
C output and income
D output only

15.9 An isolated community produces only one good, a newspaper, which sells 1,000 copies to a wholesaler at 50p per copy. The wholesaler then sells 500 copies at 70p per copy to each of the two newsagent retailers who sell the final copy to customers for £1 per copy. What is the community's weekly output?

A £500
B £700
C £1,000
D impossible to determine

15.10 Why is GDP at market prices normally higher than GDP at factor cost?

A GDP at factor cost includes exports and imports
B GDP at factor cost excludes net property income from abroad
C Taxes are normally higher than subsidies
D GDP at factor cost is normally higher than GDP at market prices

✓ Multiple choice solutions

15.1 **B**

GDP at market prices

£m	
120	consumer expenditure
+30	general government final consumption
+35	gross domestic fixed capital
+5	value of increase in stock
+20	exports
−25	imports
185	

15.2 **B**

GNP at market prices

£m	
185	GDP at market prices
+1	net property income
186	

15.3 **A**

GNP at factor cost

£m	
186	GNP at market prices
+10	subsidies
−50	taxes
146	

15.4 **A**

Net national product at factor cost

£m	
146	GNP at factor cost
−25	capital consumption
121	

15.5 **C**

$$625 \times \frac{100}{110} = 568$$

15.6 **A**

The existence of the hidden economy and voluntary labour would underestimate the real value of goods and services.

15.7 **D**

A transfer payment is an income received for which there is no corresponding output, so odd one out is D.

15.8 **D**

Double counting can appear on the output side, since the output of one industry may be the input of another.

15.9 **C**

Two methods can be used here.

Take the value added at each stage which is the output method or the value of the final product sold, so $1{,}000 \times £1 = £1{,}000$.

15.10 **C**

GDP at market prices are normally higher than GDP at factor cost because taxes are normally higher than subsidies.

The Circular Flow of Income

The Circular Flow of Income 16

Concepts and definitions questions

16.1 *The Keynesian consumption function*

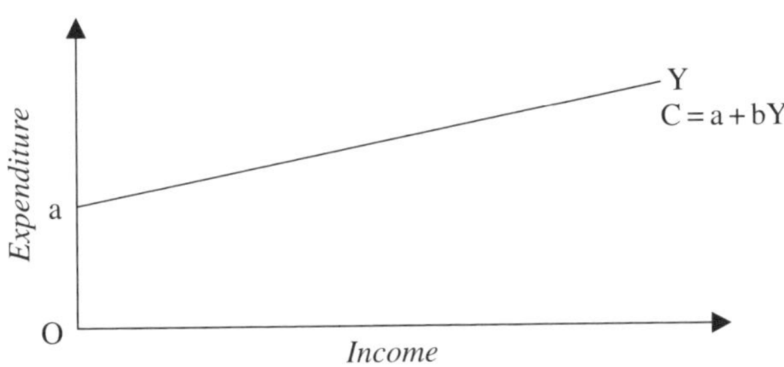

where

(i) C is
(ii) a is
(iii) b is
(iv) Y is

16.2 The Keynesian view of savings is that savings are what is left out of income after consumption. What other factors might affect the level of savings in an economy?

(i)
(ii)
(iii)
(iv)
(v)

16.3 *Marginal efficiency of investment theory*

The marginal efficiency of investment (MEI) is the rate of return expected from an investment on the last or marginal amount invested. Consider the following diagram.

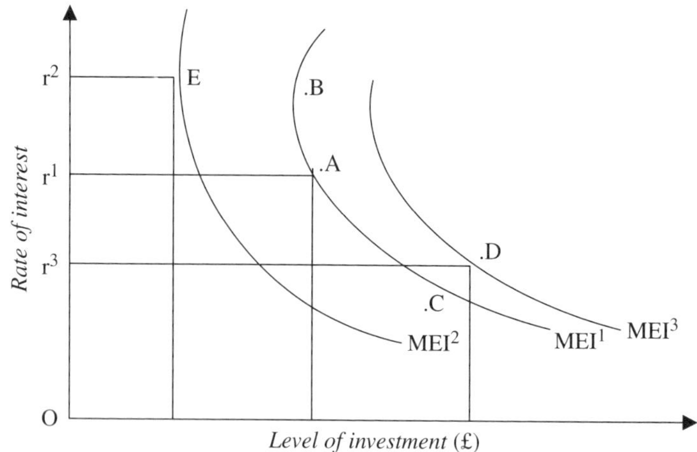

(i) On MEI1, what would cause a shift from point A to point C?
(ii) On MEI1, what would cause a shift from point A to point B?
(iii) What would cause a movement from point A to point D?
(iv) What would cause a movement from point A to point E?

16.4 *The accelerator*

The accelerator theory of investment states that an increase in consumer demand will bring about a greater increase in investment demand.

Consider the following examples.

1 A firm produces 10,000 units each year.
2 It takes 100 machines to produce 10,000 units.
3 Each machine lasts for a total of 5 years.
4 In order to maintain a regular cash flow, machines are replaced at a level of 20 per annum.
5 Each machine is working at full capacity.
6 The replacement cost of each machine is £5,000 and after 5 years it has a scrap value of zero.

Using the information in the table and your knowledge of the accelerator theory, complete the table for years 3–5.

Year	Demand	Replacement machines required	Additional machines required	Total machines required	Total investment required
1	10,000	20	–	20	£100,000
2	12,000	20	20	40	£200,000
3	14,000				
4	14,000				
5	12,000				

16.5 State three assumptions or limitations of the accelerator model.

(i)
(ii)
(iii)

16.6 What are the three injections and three withdrawals in the circular flow of income?

Injections	*Withdrawals*
(i)	(i)
(ii)	(ii)
(iii)	(iii)

16.7 (i) In a closed economy with no government sector, if current income Y is £100 million and the full employment level of Y is £125 million, how much would the government have to spend to reach the full employment level if the value of the marginal propensity to consume was equal to 0.8?

(ii) If the value of the marginal propensity to consume is 0.9, the marginal propensity to tax is 0.2 and the marginal propensity to import is 0.2, then the value of the multiplier would be

A 1
B 1.5
C 2
D impossible to determine

16.8 The paradox of thrift claims that an increase in the amount that households wish to save does not lead to an increase in the amount that is saved. How can this be possible?

16.9 *The trade cycle*

The trade cycle shows the fluctuations in the level of economic activity over a period of time.

(i) When there is a slight downturn in the level of economic activity, this is known as __________.
(ii) If the downturn continues for a longer period of time, it is known as __________.
(iii) The bottom of the trade cycle is known as the __________.
(iv) When the economy rises out of (iii) we have a period of __________.
(v) When the economy grows at a fast level we are in a __________ period.

16.10 State whether the following is true or false.

(i) MPC = change in C/change in Y.
(ii) APC = actual C/actual Y.
(iii) Higher interest rates will encourage spending.
(iv) The marginal efficiency of capital is inversely related to the rate of interest.
(v) The accelerator states that an increase in consumer demand will reduce investment demand.
(vi) Imports, taxes and savings are leakages from the circular flow of income.
(vii) Income equals expenditure at any point on the 45° line.
(viii) The multiplier is where an injection into the flow of funds raises income by more than that amount.
(ix) Demand management is advocated to counteract the trade cycle by Keynesian economists.
(x) Household saving = disposable income – consumer expenditure.

✓ Concepts and definitions solutions

16.1 (i) C = consumption
(ii) a = consumption at zero income
(iii) b = marginal propensity to consume
(iv) Y = income

16.2 (i) interest rates
(ii) wealth
(iii) taxation policy
(iv) inflation
(v) structure of population

16.3 (i) fall in interest rates
(ii) rise in interest rates
(iii) increase in business confidence
(iv) decrease in business confidence

16.4

Year	Demand	Replacement machines required	Additional machines required	Total machines required	Total investment required
1	10,000	20	–	20	£100,000
2	12,000	20	20	40	£200,000
3	14,000	20	20	40	£200,000
4	14,000	20	–	20	£100,000
5	12,000	–	–	–	–

16.5 (i) assumes firms have no spare capacity
(ii) assumes firms have funds to finance increase in demand
(iii) assumes investment decisions are based on one year's sales figures

16.6

	Injections		*Withdrawals*
(i)	investment	(i)	savings
(ii)	government expenditure	(ii)	taxation
(iii)	exports	(iii)	imports

16.7 (i) current income Y = £100 million
full employment Y = £125 million
value of MPC = 0.8

$$\text{multiplier} = \frac{1}{1 - \text{MPC}} = \frac{1}{1 - 0.8} = \frac{1}{0.2} = 5$$

Therefore government expenditure would need to rise by £5m (×5) = £25 million

(ii) In this example, multiplier $= \dfrac{1}{\text{MPW}}$

where, MPW is the marginal propensity to withdraw. Therefore,

$$\frac{1}{\text{MPW}} = \frac{1}{\text{MPS} + \text{MPT} + \text{MPZ}}$$

where, MPS is the marginal propensity to save
MPT is the marginal propensity to tax
MPZ is the marginal propensity to import.

Thus, value of multiplier $= \dfrac{1}{0.1 + 0.2 + 0.2} = \dfrac{1}{0.5} = 2$

16.8 The paradox arises since the increase in savings leads to a reduction in consumption and increase leakages from the circular flow of income.
Lower consumption will lead to lower income.
Lower income will thus lead to a fall in savings.

16.9
(i) recession
(ii) depression
(iii) trough
(iv) recovery
(v) boom

16.10
(i) True
(ii) True
(iii) False
(iv) True
(v) False
(vi) True
(vii) True
(viii) True
(ix) True
(x) True

? Multiple choice questions

16.1 The sum of the marginal propensity to consume and the marginal propensity to save must be equal to

A less than 1
B 1
C more than 1
D any amount between 0 and infinity depending upon the level of income

16.2 A closed economy with no government sector is faced with a consumption function of 100 + MY and a multiplier of 10. This may imply that

A S = 100 + 0.9Y
B C = 100 + 10Y
C C = 100 + 0.9Y
D C = 100 + 0.1Y

16.3 Which one of the following never constitutes an injection into the circular flow of income?

A government expenditure on goods and services
B the value of exports
C investment by businesses
D payment of VAT on goods and services

16.4 The diagram below shows a consumption function.

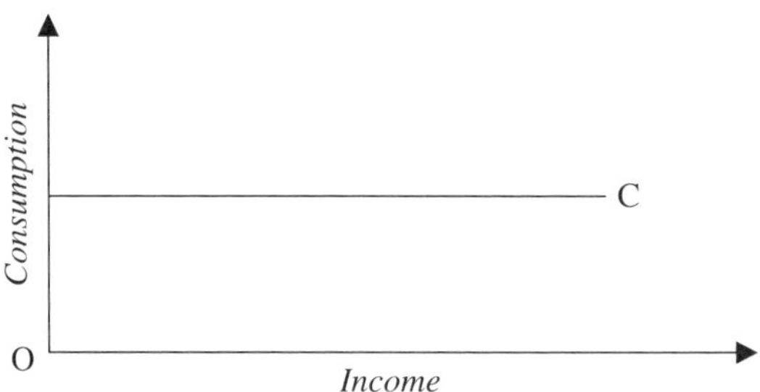

Which of the following statements is true?

A APC and MPC remain constant
B APC and MPC both fall
C APC falls, MPC remains constant
D APC remains constant, MPC falls

16.5 Consider the following information.

		£m
Exports	(X)	432
Investment	(I)	249
Savings	(S)	176
Government expenditure	(G)	329
Imports	(M)	503
Taxes	(T)	298

The national income of this economy will

A start to fall
B start to rise
C remain static
D be in equilibrium

16.6 The acceleration principle states that

A the level of investment is determined by the rate of interest
B the level of investment varies directly with the rate of change of output
C an increase in output causes inflation
D the marginal propensity to consume will rise with output

16.7 National income is in equilibrium, where

A there is a balanced budget multiplier
B planned injections = planned withdrawals
C there is full employment
D there is a balance of payments equilibrium

16.8 The figures below show the consumption function for a given economy.

Income £m	*Consumption* £m
100	95
120	110
140	125
160	140
180	155

The value of the MPC in this economy is

A 0.95
B 0.85
C 0.75
D 0.50

16.9 A closed economy with no government sector has a marginal propensity to consume of 0.8 and a full employment level of £100 million. The current level of national income is £80 million. To achieve full employment, investment must rise by

A £4 million
B £8 million
C £16 million
D £20 million

16.10 In a given economy, of each additional £1 of income, 30% is taken in as taxes, 10% is spent on imports and 50% is spent on domestically produced goods. The value of the multiplier is

A 1.5
B 2
C 2.5
D 3

✓ Multiple choice solutions

16.1 **B**

The sum of the marginal propensity to consume and the marginal propensity to save must be equal to one.

16.2 **C**

A closed economy with no government sector is faced with a consumption function of 100 + MY and a multiplier of 10 implies that C = 100 + 0.9Y.

A multiplier of 10 is consistent with an MPC = 0.9

That is $\frac{1}{1 - 0.9} = \frac{1}{0.1} = 10$

16.3 **D**

Taxation is a withdrawal from the circular flow of income.

16.4 **C**

In the diagram the APC is falling and the MPC is constant.

16.5 **B**

Injections	*Withdrawals*
£m	£m
432	176
249	503
329	298
1,010	977

Since injections are higher than withdrawals, the national income of the economy will start to rise.

16.6 **B**

The acceleration principle states that the level of investment varies directly with the rate of change of output.

16.7 **B**

National income is in equilibrium where planned injections = planned withdrawals.

16.8 **C**

Value of MPC $= \frac{\Delta C}{\Delta Y} = \frac{15}{20} = 0.75$

16.9 **A**

Income needs to rise by £20 million

Value of multiplier $= \frac{1}{1 - \text{MPC}} = \frac{1}{\text{MPS}} = \frac{1}{1 - 0.8} = \frac{1}{0.2} = 5$

So to achieve full employment, investment must rise by x × 5 to make £20 million
x = £4 million

16.10 **B**

If 30% is taken in as taxes
10% is on imports
50% on domestically produced goods, we must assume that 10% is saved

$$\text{so multiplier} = \frac{1}{\text{MPW}} = \frac{1}{0.3 + 0.1 + 0.1} = \frac{1}{0.5} = 2$$

where 0.3 = marginal propensity to tax
0.1 = marginal propensity to import
0.1 = marginal propensity to save

Inflation and Unemployment

Inflation and Unemployment

17

Concepts and definitions questions

17.1 State two sources of cost push inflation and two sources of demand pull inflation.

(i)
(ii)

17.2 Inflation may be defined as the continuous increase in the level of prices resulting in a fall in the value of a given currency. Which groups gain and lose out to inflation?

Gainers	*Losers*
(i)	(i)
(ii)	(ii)
(iii)	(iii)

17.3 What is the quantity theory of money?

17.4 State five types of unemployment.

(i)
(ii)
(iii)
(iv)
(v)

17.5 State five causes of unemployment.

(i)
(ii)
(iii)
(iv)
(v)

17.6 What is the Phillips curve?

17.7 Give six examples of supply-side policies:

(i)
(ii)
(iii)
(iv)
(v)
(vi)

17.8 What is NAIRU?

17.9 State four costs of unemployment.

(i)
(ii)
(iii)
(iv)

17.10 How do the Keynesians and monetarists disagree about the causes of unemployment?

✓ Concepts and definitions solutions

17.1 (i) *Sources of cost push inflation include*: rising import prices, increased indirect taxation, rising wages unrelated to the demand for labour.
(ii) *Sources of demand pull inflation include*: excessive monetary growth high government expenditure, high consumer expenditure, high investment expenditure and high export demand.

17.2

	Gainers		*Losers*
(i)	Borrowers	(i)	Savers
(ii)	Those with index-linked incomes	(ii)	Those on fixed incomes
(iii)	Those who invest in assets	(iii)	Those who hold cash

17.3 Quantity theory of money states that MV (the supply of money) = PT (the demand for money) where M is the money supply, V is the velocity of circulation, P is the price level and T is the transactions demand.

17.4 (i) *Seasonal* – where people are not employed all the year round, for example tourism.
(ii) *Structural* – caused by changes in the structure of an economy where the demand for some goods and services fall, for example coal and steel.
(iii) *Cyclical* – caused by a downturn in the level of economic activity, that is, the trade cycle.
(iv) *Frictional unemployment* – where people are in between jobs.
(v) *Voluntary unemployment* – where people choose not to work for whatever reason.

17.5 (i) A lack of demand for goods and services.
(ii) Where trade unions "price workers out of jobs" by high wage demands.
(iii) Long term decline of particular industries or occupations.
(iv) Where state benefits are higher than certain jobs, caused by tax rates in excess of 100%, that is, the poverty trap.
(v) High real rates of interest which will discourage investment.

17.6 Phillips curve is based on empirical research on the UK economy by LSE professor A. W. Phillips. He suggested that there was an inverse relationship between inflation and unemployment in the economy. This argument lost favour in the 1970s when a number of economies suffered from stagflation (rising prices and rising unemployment) something the Keynesians had no answer to.

17.7 Supply-side policies include:

(i) *Lower direct taxes*: By allowing people to keep more of their income they will work more hours.
(ii) *Privatisation*: Competition will encourage firms to be more efficient.
(iii) *Reduction in state benefits*: This should reduce the number of those who are voluntarily unemployed.
(iv) *Increase in the amount spent on education and training*: This should improve the efficiency of the current and future workforce.
(v) *Removal of trade union privileges*: Main impact is to reduce the price of labour.
(vi) *Competition policy*: Reducing anti-competitive behaviour by firms especially those with monopoly power.

17.8 NAIRU is the non-accelerating inflation rate of unemployment and is derived from the original Phillips curve. It is the level of unemployment where there is no tendency for inflation to accelerate or decelerate.

17.9
(i) Loss of tax revenue to the government
(ii) Loss of output
(iii) Loss of income to the unemployed
(iv) Damage to skills and confidence of the unemployed

17.10 *Keynesians* believe that unemployment is caused by insufficient demand in the economy, that is, a deflationary gap.

Monetarists believe that unemployment is caused by the supply price being too high.

Multiple choice questions

17.1 Monetarists believe that inflation is caused by

A rising import prices
B trade unions demanding higher wages
C the government allowing the money supply to rise faster than productivity
D full employment

17.2 A deflationary gap exists where

A there has been a general fall in prices
B planned expenditure exceeds the full employment level of output
C planned expenditure is below the full employment level of output
D the time it takes for government deflationary policy to work

17.3 The original Phillips curve suggests that there is

A an inverse relationship between the rate of inflation and the level of unemployment
B a direct relationship between the rate of inflation and the level of unemployment
C an inverse relationship between the rate of inflation and the money supply
D a direct relationship between the rate of inflation and the money supply

17.4 Which of the following groups gain from inflation?

(i) Those on fixed incomes
(ii) Those who have index-linked incomes
(iii) Those who hold onto cash
(iv) Those who invest in non-financial assets

A (i) and (ii)
B (i) and (iii)
C (ii) and (iii)
D (ii) and (iv)

17.5 The money rate of interest in an economy is 5%. The rate of inflation is 7%. What is the real rate of interest?

A −2%
B 2%
C 5%
D 7%

17.6 A downturn in the level of economic activity is likely to lead to which type of unemployment?

A seasonal
B frictional
C structural
D cyclical

17.7 A reduction in the demand for coal and steel is likely to lead to which type of unemployment?

A voluntary
B frictional
C structural
D cyclical

17.8 An economy has a velocity of circulation of 10. It produces 10,000 goods with an average price level of £12.50. The money supply must be

A 10,000
B 12,500
C 15,000
D 20,000

17.9 Monetarists believe that governments cause inflation. This is based on

A The Phillips curve
B The natural rate of unemployment
C The quantity theory of money
D The Marshall-Lerner condition

17.10 The poverty trap exists in this country because

A there is high unemployment
B at the lowest levels of income, marginal tax rates are in excess of 100%
C there is a North–South divide
D there is an ageing population

Multiple choice solutions

17.1 **C**

Monetarists believe that inflation is caused by governments allowing the money supply to rise at a faster rate than productivity.

17.2 **C**

A deflationary gap exists where planned expenditure is below the full employment level of output or income.

17.3 **A**

The original Phillips curve suggests that there is an inverse relationship between the rate of inflation and the level of unemployment.

17.4 **D**

The gainers from inflation are those who have index-linked incomes and those who invest in non-financial assets.

17.5 **A**

The real rate of interest = money rate of interest − rate of inflation
So 5% − 7% = −2%

17.6 **D**

A downturn in the level of economic activity is associated with the trade cycle.

17.7 **C**

A reduction in demand for any individual good, service or industry is associated with structural unemployment.

17.8 **B**

This is a test on the quantity theory of money so MV = PT
PT = £12.50 × 10,000 = 125,000
MV = ? × 10 = 125,000
12,500 × 10 = 125,000
So M is equal to 12,500

17.9 **C**

The monetarist school of thought is centred on the quantity theory of money.

17.10 **B**

The poverty trap exists because at the lowest level of income the marginal rate of tax is above 100%, that is, individuals become worse off by taking a job.

18 Fiscal Policy

Fiscal Policy 18

Concepts and definitions questions

18.1 Adam Smith outlined four canons of taxation in the first economics book "The Wealth of Nations". They are

(i)
(ii)
(iii)
(iv)

18.2 Complete the following statements:

(i) An indirect tax is levied on __________.
(ii) A direct tax is levied on __________ or __________.
(iii) A tax levied as a percentage of expenditure is an __________ __________ __________.
(iv) The proportion of tax paid increases as income and wealth rise, this is an example of a __________ tax.
(v) The proportion of tax paid decreases as income tax rises, this is an example of a __________ tax.
(vi) Tax levied on company profits are called __________ taxes.
(vii) National insurance is an example of a __________ tax.
(viii) Money received from a relative or benefactor upon their death is also subject to taxation, this is known as __________ tax.
(ix) Tax levied on property in the United Kingdom is called __________ tax.
(x) Tax paid on certain items such as petrol, tobacco and alcohol is known as __________ and __________ duty.

18.3 Over the past twenty years there has been a switch from direct to indirect taxation in the United Kingdom.

Advantages

(i)
(ii)
(iii)

Disadvantages

(i)
(ii)
(iii)

18.4 State three reasons why a government might offer a certain type of producer subsidy.

(i)
(ii)
(iii)

18.5 The Public Sector Net Cash Requirement (PSNCR), has increased over the past few years. This is due to

(i)
(ii)
(iii)
(iv)
(v)

18.6 Since 1997, the Chancellor of the Exchequer has adopted the golden rule, this is

(i)
(ii)
(iii)

18.7 What is the Fiscal stance?

18.8 Why might monetarists worry about a government running a large positive PSNCR?

18.9 What is the difference between PSNCR and the national debt?

18.10 Why are economists more concerned with the relative size of PSNCR rather than the absolute amount?

✓ Concepts and definitions solutions

18.1 (i) certainty
(ii) convenience
(iii) equitable
(iv) economy

18.2 (i) expenditure
(ii) income, wealth
(iii) *ad valorum* tax
(iv) progressive
(v) regressive
(vi) corporation
(vii) social security
(viii) inheritance
(ix) capital gains
(x) customs, excise

18.3 *Advantages*

(i) high levels of income tax are a disincentive to work
(ii) individuals have no choice but to pay income tax
(iii) high-tax payers, that is, high-income earners will relocate to low-tax countries.

Disadvantages

(i) it is regressive
(ii) it leads to a more uneven distribution of income and wealth
(iii) it pushes up prices of goods and services without adding to the value.

18.4 (i) to ensure that there is an adequate supply of essentials, for example agricultural products
(ii) to prevent unemployment
(iii) to protect producers against unfair foreign competitors.

18.5 (i) an ageing population
(ii) a rise in unemployment
(iii) increased expenditure on health and education
(iv) political commitments
(v) inflation

18.6 (i) Over the trade cycle as a whole, government current expenditure on goods, services and transfer payments should not exceed its taxation income.
(ii) Only investment expenditure may be financed by government borrowing.
(iii) The overall burden of public debt should not go above sustainable levels.

18.7 Fiscal stance refers to the effect the government budget on aggregate monetary demand in the economy. For example, if government expenditure was above taxation, the stance would be expansionary since this would raise aggregate demand.

18.8 Monetarists might worry about a large positive PSNCR for two reasons:

(i) It either expands the money supply with inflationary pressures or;
(ii) It raises interest rates, thereby crowding out private sector investment.

18.9 The PSNCR is the actual public sector borrowing requirement (PSBR) over a fiscal year. The national debt is the accumulated government debt which goes back to the 17th century and the setting up of the Bank of England.

18.10 If national income is rising over time, in real terms the absolute amount falls. Governments are more concerned about being able to finance such a deficit. It is the same for an individual. For someone earning in excess of £100,000 per annum, a £10,000 overdraft interest is not a major problem. For someone earning £10,000 per annum, it represents 100% of their actual salary and they do have a problem.

? Multiple choice questions

18.1 Which one of the following can be used by government to finance a public sector borrowing requirement (PSBR)?

A an increase in interest rates
B a rise in direct taxation
C an increase in stamp duty
D an issue of government savings certificates

18.2 The Laffer curve shows that

A governments collect more revenue if they raise taxation
B governments collect less revenue if they raise taxation
C governments crowd out the private sector if they raise taxation
D governments crowd out the private sector if they raise interest rates

18.3 A progressive tax is one where the tax payment

A rises as income increases
B falls as income increases
C is a constant proportion of expenditure
D rises at a faster rate than income increases

18.4 The Public Sector Net Cash Requirement is best described as

A the accumulated debts of the government
B the total amount borrowed by the banking sector
C the amount required to finance a balance of payments deficit
D the amount borrowed by the government and public authorities in a given period

18.5 The burden of an indirect tax will fall more heavily on the consumer when

A the greater is the price elasticity of demand for the good
B the lower is the price elasticity of demand for the good
C the greater is the income elasticity of demand for the good
D the lower is the price elasticity of supply

18.6 If the government wishes to pursue an expansionary fiscal policy it should

A increase taxes, increase government expenditure
B increase taxes, reduce government expenditure
C reduce taxes, increase government expenditure
D reduce taxes, reduce government expenditure

18.7 Which of the following is not an expenditure tax?

A VAT
B Excise Duties
C Customs Duties
D National Insurance

18.8 Which of the following is not in Adam Smith's canons of taxation?

A convenience
B equitable
C objectivity
D economy

18.9 Which of the following is not a reason why a government should have a budget deficit?

A political commitments
B an ageing population
C a downturn in the level of economic activity
D a fall in unemployment

18.10 Which of the following would not follow an increase in government borrowing according to the monetarist view?

A higher interest rates
B higher inflation
C higher economic growth
D lower investment

✓ Multiple choice solutions

18.1 **D**

Alternatives A, B and C are policies designed to correct a PSBR whereas an issue of government savings certificates could be used to finance it.

18.2 **B**

Arthur Laffer was the economic adviser to President Reagan who showed that raising tax rates actually reduced government revenue because

(i) people would work less
(ii) they would try and fiddle their taxes.

18.3 **D**

A progressive tax is one where the tax payment rises at a faster rate than income increases.

18.4 **D**

The Public Sector Net Cash Requirement is best described as the amount borrowed by the government and public authorities in a given period.

18.5 **B**

The burden of an indirect tax on a good will fall more heavily on a consumer when the demand for a good is inelastic. That is why governments tax goods such as petrol and cigarettes.

18.6 **C**

An expansionary fiscal policy involves reducing taxes and increasing expenditure, that is, reducing a withdrawal and increasing an injection.

18.7 **D**

VAT, Customs and Excise Duties are expenditure taxes, national insurance is an income tax.

18.8 **C**

The four canons of taxation are certainty, convenience, equitable and economy so odd one out is objectivity.

18.9 **D**

Alternatives A, B and C are all valid reasons why a government should have a budget deficit. A fall in unemployment should increase government revenue and reduce government expenditure.

18.10 **C**

The monetarists would argue that higher economic growth would not follow an increase in government borrowing.

19 Government Economic Policy

Government Economic Policy 19

Concepts and definitions questions

19.1 What are the four macroeconomic objectives of government?

(i)
(ii)
(iii)
(iv)

19.2 What are the main instruments of economic policy?

(i)
(ii)
(iii)
(iv)

19.3 Give four examples of supply-side policies.

(i)
(ii)
(iii)
(iv)

19.4 State four methods by which government policy could increase economic growth.

(i)
(ii)
(iii)
(iv)

19.5 State three reasons why a government might offer a firm a subsidy.

(i)
(ii)
(iii)

19.6 Distinguish between marketable and non-marketable debt.

19.7 State four reasons why demand management might be ineffective.

(i)
(ii)
(iii)
(iv)

19.8 What factors can contribute to the downturn in an economic trade cycle?

(i)
(ii)
(iii)
(iv)

19.9 What is fiscal drag?

19.10 Which of the following statements are Keynesian or monetarist beliefs?

(i) Supply creates demand.
(ii) If the laws of supply and demand are allowed to operate, then wages will adjust to the full employment level.
(iii) Fixed exchange rates make fiscal policy more effective.
(iv) Market mechanism might work in the long run but in the long run we are all dead.
(v) Inflation is the most important policy objective.
(vi) Full employment is the most important policy objective.
(vii) Monetary policy is more important than fiscal policy.

✓ Concepts and definitions solutions

19.1 (i) full employment
(ii) stable prices
(iii) economic growth
(iv) balance of payments

19.2 (i) fiscal policy
(ii) monetary policy
(iii) supply-side policy
(iv) exchange rate policy

19.3 (i) monetarism
(ii) increase training and education
(iii) privatisation
(iv) reduce direct taxation

19.4 (i) lower interest rates to encourage investment
(ii) increase capital allowances to encourage investment
(iii) encourage the sharing of technology amongst firms
(iv) lower exchange rates to promote exports

19.5 (i) to reduce unemployment
(ii) to protect from unfair competition
(iii) to help run a loss-making service that would not be provided, if left to market forces, for example rural transport

19.6 Marketable debt is any debt which is tradeable in the financial markets, for example treasury bills.

Non-marketable debts which the government issues are in the form of national savings products, such as national savings certificates or premium savings bonds.

19.7 (i) based on inaccurate information
(ii) based on out-of-date information
(iii) based on political rather than economic reasons
(iv) time lag it takes for policies to make their mark

19.8 (i) lack of business optimism
(ii) lack of consumer optimism
(iii) events in the rest of the world
(iv) inappropriate government policies

19.9 Fiscal drag happens during periods of inflation where incomes are pushed into higher tax brackets resulting in a fall in real disposable income.

19.10 (i) monetarist
(ii) monetarist
(iii) Keynesian
(iv) Keynesian
(v) monetarist
(vi) Keynesian
(vii) monetarist

? Multiple choice questions

19.1 Which of the following is never an objective of government economic policy?

A stable prices
B fiscal policy
C full employment
D balance of payments equilibrium

19.2 Which of the following is not an example of a supply-side policy?

A increased spending on training
B privatisation
C increased unemployment benefit
D reduced direct taxation

19.3 Which of the following are examples of government marketable debt?

(i) Treasury bills
(ii) Gilt-edged stocks
(iii) National savings certificates
(iv) Premium bonds

A (i) and (ii)
B (i) and (iii)
C (ii) and (iv)
D (iii) and (iv)

19.4 Which one of the following measures would be expected to reduce the level of unemployment?

A an increase in value-added tax
B a balanced budget
C a reduction in employers' national insurance contributions
D a rise in the value of the exchange rate

19.5 A television licence is an example of a

A Regressive tax
B Progressive tax
C Direct tax
D None of the above

19.6 The total yield from an indirect tax levied on a good is likely to be highest when

A demand is inelastic, supply is elastic
B demand is inelastic, supply is inelastic
C demand is elastic, supply is elastic
D demand is elastic, supply is inelastic

19.7 Which of the following government policies would not raise the long-term rate of economic growth?

A encouraging a higher level of business investment
B increasing expenditure on education and training
C providing tax relief for companies engaged in research and development
D trying to encourage a greater amount of consumers' expenditure

19.8 Governments wish to control inflation because

A it redistributes from rich to poor people
B it damages international competitiveness
C it reduces government tax revenue
D it reduces unemployment

19.9 If governments were seeking to reduce unemployment, they should

A reduce interest rates, raise taxes
B reduce interest rates, lower taxes
C increase interest rates, lower taxes
D increase interest rates, raise taxes

19.10 Which of the following is not an argument in favour of a minimum wage?

A it seeks to eliminate the poverty trap
B it seeks to prevent voluntary unemployment
C it prevents people from working below the minimum wage
D it seeks a more favourable distribution of income and wealth

✓ Multiple choice solutions

19.1 **B**

An even distribution may be desirable but it is not a current economic objective.

19.2 **C**

Supply-side policy is concerned with shifting the supply curve to the right, increasing unemployment benefit would have the opposite effect.

19.3 **A**

Treasury bills and gilt-edged stocks are examples of government marketable debt, national savings certificates are examples of non-marketable debt.

19.4 **C**

A reduction in employers' national insurance contributions would be expected to reduce the level of unemployment since it reduces the price of labour.

19.5 **A**

A television licence is an example of a regressive tax since a poor person is paying a larger share of his/her income than a rich person.

19.6 **B**

Total yield will be high when both demand and supply are inelastic since it will have big impact on price rise and small impact on quantity sold.

19.7 **D**

If consumer expenditure rises there will be less money in the long run available for investment.

19.8 **B**

Governments wish to control inflation because it damages international competitiveness.

19.9 **B**

If governments were seeking to reduce unemployment, they should reduce interest rates and lower taxes.

19.10 **C**

People who are prepared to work for below the minimum wage may be prevented from doing so if there is a minimum wage because the supply of labour is being restricted. We are talking about the economic argument here not the moral one.

The Macroeconomic Context of Business: The International Economy

Globalisation and Trade

Globalisation and Trade

20

Concepts and definitions questions

20.1 State four advantages of free trade.

(i)
(ii)
(iii)
(iv)

20.2 Distinguish between absolute and comparative advantage.

20.3 If free trade leads to a higher standard of living, suggest four reasons why countries pursue protectionist policies.

(i)
(ii)
(iii)
(iv)

20.4 State four types of protectionism.

(i)
(ii)
(iii)
(iv)

20.5 What is a multinational corporation?

20.6 What is the terms of trade?

20.7 What are the arguments against protectionism?

(i)
(ii)
(iii)

20.8 What are the benefits of direct foreign investment?

(i)
(ii)
(iii)
(iv)

20.9 What are the practical limitations of international trade?

(i)
(ii)
(iii)
(iv)

20.10 (i) Why might a country have a low terms of trade ratio?
(ii) How might government policy lead to a country having a low terms of trade ratio?

Concepts and definitions solutions

20.1 (i) greater choice of products and services
(ii) greater competition between firms and nations
(iii) economies of scale
(iv) specialisation allowing countries to develop greater skills

20.2 Country X has an absolute advantage over country Y in producing a good and it can do so using fewer resources.

Country X has a comparative advantage over country Y in producing a good when they have a lower opportunity cost of producing that good than country Y.

20.3 (i) to protect balance of payments
(ii) to protect domestic employment
(iii) to protect infant industries
(iv) for strategic reasons, for example agriculture and defence

20.4 (i) *Tariffs* – taxes on imports
(ii) *Quotas* – restrictions on imports
(iii) *Export subsidies* – subsidies on exports
(iv) *Exchange controls* – quotas on currency

20.5 A multinational corporation is a company engaged in production facilities outside their country of origin.

20.6 The terms of trade is an index of export and import prices and is calculated by the formula:

$$\frac{\text{export price index}}{\text{import price index}} \times 100$$

If the figure is above 100 it shows that export prices have risen faster than import prices.

20.7 (i) consumer choice is reduced
(ii) less competition between firms and nations
(iii) lower world economic welfare

20.8 (i) An increase in economic welfare as capital is transferred to economies where rates of return are higher.
(ii) Promotes technological transfer.
(iii) Creates employment.
(iv) Should improve balance of payments of recipient country.

20.9 (i) *Factor immobility* – unlike the model of perfect competition, factors of production do not move freely.
(ii) *Transport costs* – on bulky low value goods, there will be no advantage of specialisation and trade.
(iii) *The size of the market* – may not be big enough or ready for certain products and services.
(iv) *Government policies* – for reasons suggested in Question 20.3, governments may wish to discourage free trade.

20.10 (i) A low terms of trade ratio indicates that import prices have risen faster than export prices.

(ii) A government might favour this, since it indicates that export prices are competitive and inflation is lower. The government may have pursued restrictionary fiscal and monetary policy.

Multiple choice questions

20.1

	2004	*2005*
Export index	100	154.7
Import index	100	146.5

The terms of trade for 2005 were expected to be

A 8.2
B 54.7
C 94.4
D 105.6

20.2 The theory of comparative advantage states that

A A country will only benefit from trade in the production of a good in which it has an absolute advantage.
B A country will export labour intensive goods and import capital intensive goods.
C A country can benefit from trade even if they have an absolute disadvantage in all commodities.
D Foreign trade should be viewed with suspicion.

20.3 Which of the following is not an example of protectionism?

A Export subsidy
B Fixed exchange rate
C Import quota
D Import tariff

20.4 Why do countries impose tariffs on foreign goods?

A To prevent unemployment overseas
B To prevent unemployment at home
C To encourage free trade
D To help lesser developed countries

20.5 A customs union is

A an area of the world where you pay no tax
B an area with the same unit of currency
C a free trade area which requires fixed exchange rates between member countries
D a free trade area within a certain group of countries who have a common tariff with the rest of the world

20.6 An increase in the international mobility of factors of production leads to

A an increase in international trade
B increased unemployment in low wage economies
C increasing differences in wage rates between countries
D decreasing differences in factor prices between countries

20.7 A multinational company is best described as one which

A sells its output in more than one country
B produces goods and services in more than one country
C is owned by shareholders in more than one country
D has a product-based structure

20.8 If a country's terms of trade falls, this implies

(i) export prices have risen faster than import prices
(ii) import prices have risen faster than export prices
(iii) the country needs to sell foreign exchange reserves

A (i) and (iii)
B (ii) and (iii)
C (i) only
D (ii) only

20.9 Which of the following statements is false?

A International trade allows countries to specialise
B International trade allows consumers to a wider range of goods and services
C International trade brings about economies of scale
D International trade leads to international competition and higher prices

20.10 In country A it takes 10 hours of labour to make one unit of x and 5 hours to make one unit of y.

In country B it takes 6 hours of labour to make one unit of x and 9 hours to make one unit of y.

Which of the following statements is correct?

A Country A has a comparative advantage in the production of both goods.
B Country B has an absolute advantage in the production of x and country A has a comparative advantage in the production of good x.
C Country B has an absolute advantage in the production of both goods.
D Country A has an absolute advantage in the production of both goods.

✓ Multiple choice solutions

20.1 **D**

Terms of trade is $\frac{154.7}{146.5} \times 100$

$=105.6$

20.2 **C**

The theory of comparative advantage states that a country can benefit from trade even if they have an absolute disadvantage in all commodities.

20.3 **B**

Alternatives A, C and D are all examples of protectionism. A fixed exchange rate is a type of exchange rate.

20.4 **B**

A country imposes tariffs on foreign goods to protect employment at home.

20.5 **D**

A customs union is a free trade area within a certain group of countries who have a common tariff with the rest of the world.

20.6 **D**

An increase in the international mobility of factors of production leads to decreasing differences in factor prices between countries.

20.7 **B**

A multinational company is best described as one which produces goods and services in more than one country.

20.8 **D**

If a country's terms of trade falls, this implies that import prices have risen faster than export prices.

20.9 **D**

Alternatives A, B and C are all correct. Statement D is half correct, increased competition should lead to lower prices.

20.10 **B**

Country B has an absolute advantage in the production of good x so we can eliminate alternatives A and D.

However, country B does not have an absolute advantage in the production of good y so we can eliminate C.

Therefore, by process of elimination, the answer is B.

Foreign Exchange

Foreign Exchange 21

Concepts and definitions questions

21.1 Supply and demand for sterling against dollar/sterling exchange rate

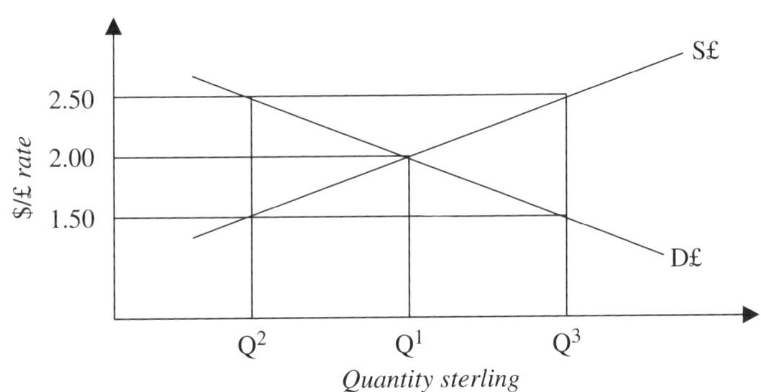

(i) At an exchange rate of $2.50 – £1 is sterling over or under valued?
(ii) If $2.50 – £1 was the fixed exchange rate would the Bank of England have to buy or sell sterling in the foreign exchange markets?
(iii) What quantity would they have to buy/sell?
(iv) What is the market rate of sterling against the dollar?

21.2 State three advantages of floating exchange rates.

(i)
(ii)
(iii)

21.3 State three disadvantages of floating exchange rates.

(i)
(ii)
(iii)

21.4 What is a managed or a dirty float?

21.5 What is the purchasing power parity theory?

21.6 What are the economic forces and other factors which determine the demand for and supply of currencies?

(i)
(ii)
(iii)
(iv)
(v)
(vi)

21.7 In order to join the single currency, what was the convergence criteria member states had to fulfil?

(i)
(ii)
(iii)
(iv)

21.8 What is the overriding advantage and disadvantage of joining the single currency?

(i) *Advantage* –
(ii) *Disadvantage* –

21.9 What is the J curve and what is it caused by?

21.10 State whether the following statements are true or false.

(i) The terms of trade are the ratio of an index of export prices to an index of import prices.
(ii) If the terms of trade deteriorate we need to sell less exports.
(iii) Free trade can benefit a country even if it has an absolute disadvantage in the production of the two commodities it produces.
(iv) Governments determine exchange rates under floating exchange rates.
(v) The main argument in favour of a single currency is that it will reduce transaction costs within member countries.
(vi) A country suffering from a deficit on capital account in the balance of payments and inflation should increase interest rates.
(vii) International trade leads to increased competition and higher prices.
(viii) The imposition of a tariff on an imported car should lead to an increase in price and a reduction in the number bought.
(ix) Imports are an injection in the circular flow of income.
(x) A balance of payments surplus in the UK will lead to an increase in demand for sterling.

Concepts and definitions solutions

21.1 (i) overvalued
(ii) buy
(iii) $Q^2 - Q^3$
(iv) \$2 = £1

21.2 (i) Monetary policy becomes more effective
(ii) Automatic adjustment to balance of payments surplus or deficit
(iii) Exchange rate becomes instrument not objective of policy

21.3 (i) Uncertainty makes trade more difficult
(ii) Fiscal policy becomes ineffective
(iii) Depreciation on its own may not correct a deficit

21.4 A managed or dirty float is where a government allows the market to dictate exchange rates on a day-to-day basis but governments will intervene if they think exchange rate is too high or too low.

21.5 The purchasing power parity theory states that the value of an exchange rate should reflect what that currency can buy, for example if a Big Mac costs \$2 in New York and the exchange rate is \$2 = £1 then a Big Mac in London should cost £1.

21.6 (i) relative inflation rates
(ii) trade flows
(iii) investment flows
(iv) economic prospects
(v) speculator's judgement
(vi) technical analysis

21.7 (i) Inflation should be within 1.5 percentage points of the average of the three best performing members for a period of one year.
(ii) Government deficits should not exceed 3 per cent of GDP.
(iii) A 2.25% narrow band for their currency, without initiating a realignment for at least two years.
(iv) Long-term interest rates must be within 2 percentage points of the three best performing states, in terms of price stability.

21.8 (i) *Advantage* – reduction in transaction costs
(ii) *Disadvantage* – loss of control of domestic monetary policy, that is interest rates

21.9 The J curve is where a country devalues and finds that, in the short run, the deficit actually gets larger on the balance of payments.

This is caused by the time lag it takes for people to adjust their spending patterns.

21.10 (i) True
(ii) False
(iii) True
(iv) False
(v) True
(vi) True
(vii) False
(viii) True
(ix) False
(x) True

Multiple choice questions

21.1 The J curve effect is caused by

A cost-push inflation
B international trade barriers
C change in interest rates
D the time it takes consumers to adjust their spending habits following a revaluation or devaluation of a currency

21.2 The main advantage of a system of flexible or floating exchange rates is that it:

A provides certainty for those engaged in international trade
B provides automatic correction of balance of payments
C reduces international transaction costs
D provides discipline for government economic management

21.3 Which of the following is not a function of the World Trade Organisation (WTO)?

A providing finance for countries with a balance of payments deficit
B encouraging countries to reduce tariffs
C encouraging free trade areas
D discouraging non-tariff barriers

21.4 A devaluation of the exchange rate for a country's currency will normally result in

(i) a reduction in the current account deficit
(ii) an improvement in the country's terms of trade
(iii) a reduction in the domestic cost of living
(iv) an increased level of domestic economic activity

A (i) and (ii) only
B (i) and (iv) only
C (ii) and (iii) only
D (ii) and (iv) only

21.5 Which of the following is not a benefit of a single currency?

A reduced transaction costs
B lower interest rates
C reduced exchange rate uncertainty
D increased price transparency

21.6 Which one of the following would likely lead to a fall in the value of sterling against the dollar?

A a rise in UK interest rates
B a rise in US interest rates
C the Bank of England buying sterling for dollars
D capital investment flows from New York to London

21.7 The current rate of exchange between the UK and the United States is £1 = $1.50. The sterling price of a Jaguar car is £100,000. If the exchange rate moves to £1 = $1.40 and the sterling price remains the same, what will be the new dollar price of the car?

A $100,000
B $140,000
C $150,000
D $160,000

21.8 The major disadvantage of a single currency to an individual country is:

A loss of monetary control
B loss of fiscal control
C higher transaction costs
D none of the above

21.9 Which one of the following shows the lowest degree of international mobility within Europe?

A management
B capital
C technology
D unskilled labour

21.10 The advantage of fixed exchange rates include:

(i) monetary policy is more effective
(ii) fiscal policy is more effective
(iii) there will be no need to hold reserves

A (i) and (ii)
B (i) and (iii)
C (ii) and (iii)
D (ii) only

Multiple choice solutions

21.1 **D**

The J curve effect is caused by the time it takes consumers to adjust their spending habits following a revaluation or devaluation of a currency.

21.2 **B**

The main advantage of a system of flexible or floating exchange rates is that it provides automatic correction of balance of payments.

21.3 **A**

Providing finance for countries with a balance of payments deficit is not a function of GATT.

21.4 **B**

A devaluation of the exchange rate for a country's currency will normally result in a reduction in the current account deficit and an increase in the level of economic activity.

21.5 **B**

A single currency does not necessarily ensure lower interest rates.

21.6 **B**

A rise in American interest rates is likely to make funds flow from the UK to the United States which would lead to a fall in the value of sterling.

21.7 **B**

If sterling equals £1 to $1.50 a £100,000 car would be $150,000. A reduction in sterling to £1 = $1.40 would reduce the dollar price by $10,000 to $140,000.

21.8 **A**

The major disadvantage of a single currency to an individual country is loss of monetary control.

21.9 **D**

The least mobile factor of production with regard to mobility within Europe is unskilled labour.

21.10 **D**

The only advantage of fixed exchange rates listed here is that fiscal policy is more effective.

22 Balance of Payments

Balance of Payments

22

Concepts and definitions questions

22.1 The balance of payments is a financial record of transactions between individuals, companies and government of one country with that of another. For the United Kingdom, it is customary to measure these figures over a calendar year. It is comprised of the following sections:

(i) The ___________ account relates to tangible goods.
(ii) The ___________ account relates to services, interest, profit and dividends.
(iii) If we add together (i) and (ii) this gives us the ___________ account.
(iv) Cross border changes in the holding of assets and liabilities is recorded in the ___________ account of the balance of payments.
(v) If these totals do not add up properly there is an adjustment made which is called either the ___________ ___________ or ___________ ___________.

22.2 The following figures are available to you:

Exports	£10 million
Imports	£12 million
Invisible trade credit	£6 million
Debit	£5 million
Capital account balance	£500,000 inflow

(i) Calculate the visible trade balance
(ii) Calculate the invisible balance
(iii) Calculate the balance on the combined current and capital account

22.3 Define the following terms.

(i) Visible earnings
(ii) Invisible trade
(iii) Current account deficit
(iv) Errors and omissions

22.4 What is hot money?

22.5 State three items which would appear as a surplus on the UK invisible balance.

(i)
(ii)
(iii)

22.6 Calculate the current account balance for the following 3 years.

	Visible balance £m	*Invisible balance* £m
Year 1	−13,771	+2,972
Year 2	−13,378	+2,706
Year 3	−10,594	+8,411

(i) Current account year 1 =
(ii) Current account year 2 =
(iii) Current account year 3 =

22.7 What is deindustrialisation?

22.8 What policy options can a government take if it is faced with a balance of payments deficit?

(i)
(ii)
(iii)
(iv)

22.9 What is the Marshall-Lerner condition?

22.10 Why are governments reluctant to use deflation to solve a balance of payments disequilibrium?

✓ Concepts and definitions solutions

22.1 (i) visible
(ii) invisible
(iii) current
(iv) financial
(v) balancing item, statistical error

22.2 (i) −£2 million (10 − 12)
(ii) +£1 million (6 − 5)
(iii) −£2 million + £1 million + £500,000 = −£500,000

22.3 (i) Visible earnings are our exports on tangible goods such as cars, textiles and foodstuffs.
(ii) Invisible trade is trade in services such as shipping, banking and insurance.
(iii) A current account deficit is where a combination of the visible and invisible balance is negative.
(iv) Since the balance of payments as a whole always balances to zero any apparent imbalance must be due to errors and omissions in the accounts. Thus a figure that balances the accounts to zero is entered under this heading.

22.4 Hot money is not stolen money! It is money which moves from one capital centre to the next if the owners can achieve a higher rate of return elsewhere.

22.5 (i) airlines
(ii) insurance
(iii) banking

22.6 (i) 10,799 deficit
(ii) 10,672 deficit
(iii) 2,183 deficit

22.7 *Deindustrialisation* is the absolute loss of jobs in the manufacturing sector of an economy. It has also been described as a country's inability to maintain full employment and a balance of payments equilibrium.

22.8 (i) *Devaluation* – makes exports cheaper and imports more expensive
(ii) *Tariffs* – make imports more expensive
(iii) *Quotas* – restrict imports
(iv) *Export subsidies* – give subsidies to export-producing industries

22.9 The Marshall-Lerner condition states that for a devaluation to work the combined sum of the price elasticities of demand for exports and imports must be greater than 1.

22.10 Governments are reluctant to use deflation to solve a balance of payments problem because deflationary policies are unpopular because they lead to reduced spending and unemployment. In a democracy that is no way for governments to be re-elected.

Multiple choice questions

22.1 If the elasticity of demand for British exports is −2, then a devaluation of sterling should lead to

A a fall in the value of exports
B an increase in the value of imports
C an increase in the total foreign currency expenditure on British goods
D British goods becoming more expensive overseas

22.2 Consider the following figures

Tangible exports	£35,432 million
Tangible imports	£36,607 million
Invisible balance	£1,429 million
Current account	£354 million
Capital account	£−2,227 million

The visible trade balance was:

A −£1,175 million
B +£254 million
C −£1,126 million
D +£1,973 million

22.3 Which of the following must always balance?

A The balancing item
B The invisible balance
C The balance on current account
D The balance of payments

22.4 ICI based in the UK have a subsidiary in France. Last year this French subsidiary made £10 million profit of which £5 million was invested in France and the remainder came back to the UK. They decide to invest a further £15 million in France of which £10 million came from the parent company and £5 million was raised in France. The total currency flow for the UK was

A an outflow of £10 million
B an inflow of £10 million
C an outflow of £5 million
D an inflow of £5 million

22.5 The marginal propensity to import is

A an increase in import prices following a devaluation
B price index of exports divided by price index of imports
C the proportion of imports to exports
D the relationship between a change in income and the consequent change in imports

22.6 Which one of the following will appear in the financial account of the balance of payments?

A The export of whisky
B The purchase of Euros to go on a Spanish holiday
C Interest received on a United States government bond
D Inflow of investment by Sony into the UK

22.7 A balance of payments deficit is least likely to be corrected by

A imposing tariffs
B increasing the value of sterling
C reducing the level of aggregate demand
D discouraging imports

22.8 The following table gives information about the visible trade of a certain country

	Exports	
	Average price per unit	**Units sold**
Year 1	£200	1,000
Year 2	£400	800

Between years 1 and 2 what changes have taken place in the balance of trade and the terms of trade?

	Balance of trade	*Terms of trade*
A	improved	worsened
B	improved	improved
C	worsened	worsened
D	worsened	improved

22.9 Which of the following would not be included in the UK balance of payments statistics?

A The terms of trade
B The takeover of a UK company by a German company
C The purchase of a villa in Spain by a UK citizen
D The UK government borrowing money from another central bank

22.10 Which of the following statements about balance of payments is not correct

A Payments that lead to demands for foreign currency are measured As debits while payments that lead to supplies of foreign exchange Are measured as credits.
B The current account balance plus the capital and financial account Balances add up to zero.
C a current account deficit indicates a week economy as only healthy Ones have a current account surplus
D a current account surplus implies that domestic residents are Increasing their Net foreign assets

Multiple choice solutions

22.1 **C**

If the elasticity of demand for British exports is −2, then a devaluation of sterling should lead to an increase in the total foreign currency expenditure on British goods.

22.2 **A**

Tangible exports	£35,432
Tangible imports	£36,607
=	−£1,175

22.3 **D**

The balance of payments must always balance. Even if there is a balance of payments deficit, there is a balance for official financing.

22.4 **C**

Profits from France	+£5 million
Investment in France	−£10 million
Outflow of	£5 million

22.5 **D**

The marginal propensity to import is the relationship between a change in income and the consequent change in imports.

22.6 **D**

A is a visible transaction
B is an invisible transaction
C is an invisible transaction
D is a capital flow

22.7 **B**

A balance of payments deficit is least likely to be corrected by increasing the value of sterling.

22.8 **B**

The balance of trade improved because export earnings rose from £2 million to £3.2 million. The terms of trade improved because average export prices increased.

22.9 **A**

The terms of trade is a price index of exports to imports so would not be included in UK balance of payments statistics.

22.10 **C**

A current account deficit is often a sign of an economy which is growing fast.

Mock Assessment

Mock Assessment

Mock Assessment 1

Paper CO4
Fundamentals of Business Economics

Instructions: attempt all 75 questions

Time allowed 2 hours

Do not turn the page until you are ready to attempt the assessment under timed conditions

Mock Assessment – Questions

Question 1

Which ONE of the following would lead directly to an outward shift in a country's production possibility frontier?

(A) A rise in the population of working age.
(B) A fall in unemployment.
(C) An increase in outward migration.
(D) A rise in the school leaving age.

(2 marks)

Question 2

The cost of one good or service measured in terms of what must be sacrificed to obtain it is called:

(A) real cost.
(B) potential cost.
(C) opportunity cost.
(D) social cost.

(2 marks)

Question 3

The following financial data refers to a company.

Capital employed	1.1.06	$900000
Capital employed	31.12.06	$1100000
Gross profits for year ending	31.12.06	105000
Interest payments year ending	31.12.06	20000
Tax paid on profits year ending	31.12.06	15000

What is the value of the rate of return on capital for this company?

(2 marks)

Question 4

All of the following are essential features of a market economy EXCEPT which ONE?

(A) Private ownership of productive resources.
(B) Allocation of resources by the price mechanism.
(C) Absence of entry and exit barriers to and from industries.
(D) Prices determined by market forces.

(2 marks)

Question 5

Consider the following data for business:

Output	*Fixed Cost*	*Total Variable Cost*	*Marginal Revenue*
10	$100	$150	$12
11	$100	$164	$12
12	$100	$176	$12
13	$100	$199	$12
14	$100	$236	$12
15	$100	$275	$12

From this data you are required to calculate for this business:

(A) the average cost of production at output level 10.
(B) the marginal cost of production at output level 11.
(C) the optimum level of output for this business.
(D) the profit maximising level of output for this business.

(4 marks)

Question 6

A business will maximise profits only if it produces where:

(A) average cost = marginal revenue.
(B) marginal cost = marginal revenue.
(C) average cost = average revenue.
(D) marginal cost = average revenue.

(2 marks)

Question 7

Consider the following data for a proposed investment project.

Capital cost of the project	$7000
Life of the investment	3 years
Scrap value of the capital at end of Year 3	$500
Income generated by the project	
Year 1	$2000
Year 2	$3000
Year 3	$2000

From this data you are required to calculate:

(a) The net present value for the project assuming a discount rate of 10%

(2 marks)

(b) Is this project profitable for the company? yes/no

(1 mark)

(c) The net present value for the project assuming a discount rate of 6% and a final scrap value of $1000

(2 marks)

Question 8

The price earnings ratio is measured by:

(A) Dividing earnings per share by the market price of the share.
(B) Dividing the current market price of the share by the earnings per share.
(C) Dividing the earnings per share by the rate of discount.
(D) Dividing the current market price of the share by total profits.

(2 marks)

Question 9

All of the following would be expected to raise share values EXCEPT which one?

(A) An announcement of higher than expected profits.
(B) A reduction in corporation tax.
(C) A rise in interest rates.
(D) A rise in share prices on overseas stock markets.

(2 marks)

Question 10

The . . . (i)........ in a company are all those who have an interest in the strategy and behaviour of the . . . (ii)........ Their interest may not always coincide with those of the . . . (iii)........ who are principally interested in . . . (iv)........ The task of . . . . (v)........ is to attempt to reconcile these conflicting interests.

Read the above passage and indicate where each of the following words should be placed in the passage.

(A) Management
(B) Shareholders
(C) Stakeholders
(D) Company
(E) Profits

(5 marks)

Question 11

State whether each of the following statements about limited liability companies are true or false.

Statement	True	False
(i) Shareholders are not liable for the debts of the company.		
(ii) Owners always exercise day-to-day decision making authority.		
(iii) Owners share in the profits of the company, but not necessarily in proportion to the number of shares that they own.		

(3 marks)

Question 12

The principal–agent problem refers to:

(A) situations where a company's selling agents are not meeting the company's main sales targets.
(B) problems arising when a principal delegates authority to an agent but cannot ensure the agent will always act in his/her interest.
(C) cases where companies lack knowledge on particular markets and have to seek agents to act on their behalf.
(D) the power a large company may exert over supplier's when it is the dominant buyer of that supplier's output.

(2 marks)

Question 13

For each of the following economic processes, indicate whether the effect on the *short run average cost* for a firm would be to raise the cost curve, lower the cost curve or to leave the cost curve unaffected.

Economic process	Raise curve	Lower curve	Leave curve unaffected
A rise in wage costs			
Increase opportunities for economies of scale.			
A fall in the price of raw materials			
A shift in the demand curve to the left			

(4 marks)

Question 14

Indicate whether each of the following statements is *true* or *false*.

Statement	True	False
The law of diminishing returns shows how long run cost tends to rise if the scale of output becomes too great		
A firm's short run cost curve is always U shaped; the long cost curve may or may not be		
For most firms technological change is one of the most important economies of scale		
Economies of scale act as barrier to entry to industries.		

(4 marks)

Question 15

Indicate whether each of the following are typical characteristics of an oligopoly market (yes/no).

Characteristic	Yes	No
A large number of small firms		
A preference for non-price competition over price competition		
Interdependence of decision making		
Ease of entry and exit to and from the industry.		

(4 marks)

Question 16

State whether each of the following statements is *true* or *false*.

Statement	True	False
Collusion is more likely in oligopoly markets than in other markets		
If there are economies of scale, a monopoly firm may charge lower prices than equivalent firms facing competition		
Oligopolistic firms can never achieve lower long run costs than could competitive firms in the same industry		
Oligopolistic firms can make excess profits but only in the short run.		

(4 marks)

Question 17

If a business currently sells 10,000 units of its product per month at $10 per unit and the demand for its product has a price elasticity of −2.5, a rise in the price of the product to $11 will:

(A) raise total revenue by $7,250.
(B) reduce total revenue by $17,500.
(C) reduce total revenue by $25,000.
(D) raise total revenue by $37,500.

(2 marks)

Question 18

In the kinked demand curve model of oligopoly, the kink in the firm's demand curve is due to the firm's belief that competitors will:

(A) set a price at the kink of the demand curve.
(B) will match all price increases and price reductions.
(C) will match any price increases, but not any price reductions.
(D) will match any price reductions, but not any price increases.

(2 marks)

Question 19

Which ONE of the following is a natural barrier to the entry of new firms into an industry?

(A) Large initial capital costs.
(B) The issuing of patents.
(C) A government awarded franchise.
(D) The licensing of professions.

(2 marks)

Question 20

The following data refers to an industry consisting of 6 companies.

Company	Sales	Market Share
No 1	1200	
No 2	800	
No 3	600	
No 4	600	
No 5	500	
No 6	500	
No 7	450	
No 8	350	
The four-firm concentration ratio		

You are required to calculate:
(a) the market shares for each company.
(b) the four-firm concentration ratio for this industry.

(3 marks)

Question 21

If the market supply curve for a good is inelastic, an increase in demand will:

(A) Raise total sales proportionately more than it will raise the market price.
(B) Raise total sales proportionately less than it will raise the market price.
(C) Raise the market price but leave total sales unaffected.
(D) Raise total sales but leave the market price unchanged.

(2 marks)

Question 22

Mergers between businesses engaged in the same stage of production of a similar good or service are known as:

(A) Horizontal mergers.
(B) Conglomerate mergers.
(C) Vertical mergers.
(D) Cross mergers.

(2 marks)

Question 23

A good which is characterised by both rivalry and excludability is called:

(A) a public good.
(B) a private good.
(C) a government good.
(D) an external good.

(2 marks)

Question 24

The burden of an indirect tax on a good will fall more heavily on the producer when:

(A) demand for the good is price elastic.
(B) demand for the good is price inelastic.
(C) demand for the good has unit elasticity.
(D) supply of the good is price elastic.

(2 marks)

Question 25

In practice a monopoly may have its market power limited by all of the following EXCEPT which ONE?

(A) Countervailing power from its customers.
(B) The market may be contestable.
(C) There may be close substitutes for the good.
(D) The firm's long run average cost curve may be falling.

(2 marks)

Question 26

The following is a list of possible sources of market failure.

(i) Externalities
(ii) Monopoly power
(iii) Public goods and services
(iv) Merit goods
(v) Monopsony power
(vi) Lack of knowledge

For each of the following cases, indicate which one of the above sources of market failure matches the case given:

(A) Businesses fail to properly train their employees because they fear that they will move to other firms after their training.
(B) There is a failure to provide efficient street cleaning services because it is impossible for the service providers to ensure that all who benefited from the services paid for them.
(C) Employers pay their workers wages which are below their productivity – their marginal revenue product.
(D) A company's marginal revenue is not equal to the price of the good it produces and it therefore does not equate price with marginal cost.

(2 marks)

? Question 27

Which ONE of the following is the best example of a merit good?

(A) Street lighting.
(B) A national defence force.
(C) Company cars for top sales executives.
(D) A system of public libraries.

(2 marks)

? Question 28

There are three types of mergers

(i) Horizontal mergers
(ii) Vertical mergers
(iii) Conglomerate mergers

Match the following reasons for a merger with the appropriate type of merger listed above.

(A) To increase monopoly power and control over the market.
(B) To ensure control over supplies of raw materials and components.
(C) To secure economies of scale.
(D) To reduce risk by diversifying the range of products sold and the range of markets.

(4 marks)

? Question 29

State whether the following statements about the privatisation of state industries are true or false.

Statement	True	False
(i) Privatisation increases the commercial pressure on the business to make a profit.		
(ii) Privatisation ensures the business faces competition and so encourages greater efficiency.		
(iii) Privatisation is a means of solving the principal–agent problem.		
(iv) Privatisation is likely to make the business more responsive to needs of its customers.		

(4 marks)

Question 30

Which of the following are features of monopolistic competition?

(i) Large numbers of producers in the industry.
(ii) Differentiated products.
(iii) Companies producing at less than optimum output.
(iv) Monopoly profits in the long run.

(A) (i), (iii) and (iv) only.
(B) (ii), (iii) and (iv).
(C) (i), (ii) and (iii) only.
(D) (i), (ii) and (iv) only.

(2 marks)

Question 31

The cobweb theorem:

(A) shows that, without intervention some agricultural prices will fall continuously over time.
(B) explains why some agricultural prices are characterised by instability from one year to another.
(C) shows that when some agricultural prices are disturbed, prices steadily return to their equilibrium level.
(D) the imposition of minimum prices in agricultural products always lead to unsold surpluses.

(2 marks)

Question 32

The following diagram shows the cost and revenue curves for a monopoly firm. The firm is producing at output level Q1.

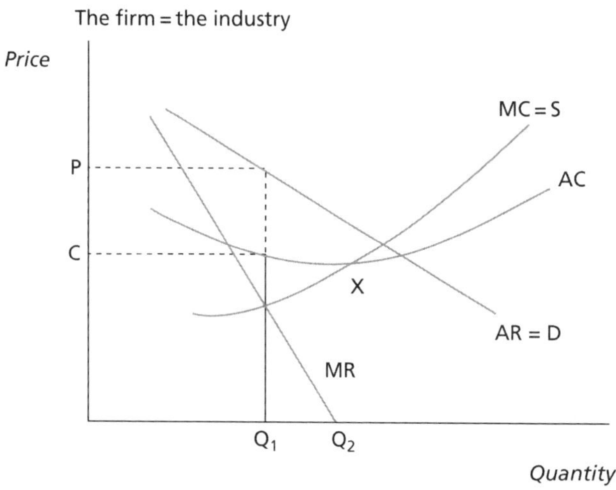

You are required to:

(a) State whether the firm is producing at, above or below the optimum level of output. at/above/below

(b) State whether the firm is producing at, above or below the profit maximising level of output. at/above/below.

(c) Identify the abnormal (monopoly) profits the firm is currently earning.

(3 marks)

Question 33

The necessary conditions for a firm to be able to practice price discrimination are:

(i) The firm must be a price setter.
(ii) The markets must be kept separate.
(iii) The price elasticity of demand must be different in each market.
(iv) Customers in each market must not be aware of the prices changed in other markets.

(A) (i), (ii) and (iii) only.
(B) (i), (ii) and (iv) only.
(C) (ii), (iii) and (iv) only.
(D) all of them.

(2 marks)

Question 34

If an indirect tax is imposed on a good or service:

(A) The price will rise by an amount equal to the tax.
(B) The producer decides on how much of the tax to pass on to the customer.
(C) The price rise will be smaller the greater is the price elasticity of demand.
(D) The price rise will be greater the smaller is the price elasticity of supply.

(2 marks)

Question 35

All of the following are examples of where externalities are likely to occur EXCEPT which ONE?

(A) A business providing training schemes for its employees.
(B) Government expenditure on vaccination programmes for infectious diseases.
(C) Attending a concert given by a government funded orchestra.
(D) Private motorists driving cars in city centres.

(2 marks)

Question 36

Whenever government intervention prevents prices from reaching their equilibrium level, the result will always include ALL of the following EXCEPT which ONE?

(A) Shortages or surpluses.
(B) Demand and supply not equal.
(C) Reduced profits for producers.
(D) Resources not allocated by price.

(2 marks)

Question 37

A rise in the price of a good accompanied by a fall in the quantity sold would result from

(A) a decrease in supply.
(B) an increase in demand.
(C) a decrease in demand.
(D) an increase in supply.

(2 marks)

Question 38

If the demand curve for Good A shifts to the left when the price of Good B rises, we may conclude that

(A) the goods are substitutes.
(B) Good A is an inferior good.
(C) the goods are complements.
(D) the demand for Good A is price elastic.

(2 marks)

Question 39

The introduction of a national minimum wage will lead a business to reduce its number of employees most when

(A) the demand for its final product is price elastic.
(B) wage costs are a small proportion of total costs.
(C) there is a low degree of substitutability between capital and labour.
(D) the supply of substitute factors of production is price inelastic.

(2 marks)

Question 40

The following is a list of different types of market structure.

- Perfect competition
- Monopolistic competition
- Oligopoly
- Monopoly

Match to each of the following situations the market structure that is being described.

Situation	Market Structure
(i) In the long run, abnormal profits are competed away by the entry of new firms and for each firm output will be the optimum level of output.	
(ii) The behaviour of any one firm is conditioned by how it expects its competitors to react to its price and output decisions.	

(2 marks)

Question 41

Which one of the following is NOT a characteristic of not-for-profit organisations?

(A) They need efficient and effective management.
(B) They make financial surpluses and deficits.
(C) They have a range of stakeholders.
(D) The absence of any principal–agent problem.

(2 marks)

Question 42

In order to finance an excess of expenditure over taxation receipts, a government could:

(A) reduce its current expenditure.
(B) issue government bonds.
(C) raise income tax.
(D) run an overdraft on its account with the World Bank.

(2 marks)

Question 43

A business could use all of the following to finance a lack of synchronisation in its short-term payments and receipts EXCEPT which ONE?

(A) a bank overdraft.
(B) trade credit.
(C) its cash reserves.
(D) a hire purchase agreement.

(2 marks)

Question 44

A risk that an organisation may not be able to realise its assets to meet a commitment associated with financial instruments is known as:

(A) credit risk.
(B) liquidity risk.
(C) interest rate risk.
(D) currency risk.

(2 marks)

Question 45

State whether each of the following financial instruments appearing on a commercial bank's balance sheet is an asset or liability for the bank.

Instrument	Asset	Liability
Advances		
Money at call with discount houses		
Deposit accounts		
Shareholder capital		

(4 marks)

Question 46

If banks are required to keep a reserve assets ratio of 10% and also wish to keep a margin of liquid reserves of 10%, by how much would deposits ultimately rise by if they acquire an additional $1000 of reserve assets?

(A) $10000
(B) $5000
(C) $1000
(D) $500

(2 marks)

Question 47

If a commercial bank reallocates some of its assets from less profitable to more profitable ones,

(A) the bank's liquidity will be increased.
(B) the safety of the bank's assets will be increased.
(C) the bank's liquidity will be decreased.
(D) the liquidity and safety of the bank's assets will be unaffected.

(2 marks)

Question 48

Which of the following statements about the relationship between bond prices and bond yields is true?

(A) They vary positively.
(B) They vary inversely.
(C) They vary inversely or positively depending on business conditions.
(D) They are not related.

(2 marks)

Question 49

Read the following passage.

A business will need to insure itself against a range of risks. It can do so by employing a ......(i)... to seek out the most appropriate insurance policies. If the risks involved are very large the insurance company ......(ii)...... the risk may engage in ...(iii)...... the risk with other companies.

You are required to indicate which of the following words should be placed in each of the gaps in the passage.

(a) Broker
(b) General insurance company
(c) Reinsuring
(d) Underwriting
(e) Assuring

(3 marks)

Question 50

Under a regime of flexible exchange rates, which one of the following would lead to a rise in the exchange rate for a country's currency?

(A) a shift in the country's balance of payments current account towards a surplus.
(B) a rise in interest rates in other countries.
(C) an increasing balance of trade deficit.
(D) the central bank buying foreign exchange on the foreign exchange market.

(2 marks)

Question 51

Exchange rates are determined by supply and demand for currencies in the foreign exchange market. State whether each of the following would be part of the supply of a country's currency or part of the demand for that country's currency.

Statement	Supply	Demand
Payments for imports into the country.		
Inflows of capital into the country.		
Purchases of foreign currency by the country's central bank.		

(2 marks)

Question 52

Each of the following is a source of funds for capital investment for business except one. Which ONE is the EXCEPTION?

(A) Commercial banks.
(B) Internally generated funds.
(C) The stock market
(D) The central bank.

(2 marks)

Question 53

The linking of net savers with net borrowers is known as:

(A) the savings function.
(B) financial intermediation.
(C) financial regulation.
(D) a store of value.

(2 marks)

Question 54

If a consumer price index rises, it shows that

(A) the value of the currency has increased.
(B) real consumer income has fallen.
(C) all prices in the economy have risen.
(D) the purchasing power of money has decreased.

(2 marks)

Question 55

The main function of the money market is to

(A) enable businesses and governments to obtain liquidity.
(B) encourage saving.
(C) permit the efficient buying and selling of shares.
(D) deal in credit instruments of more than one year maturity.

(2 marks)

Question 56

The effects of low real interest rates include all of the following EXCEPT which ONE?

(A) Credit based sales will tend to be high.
(B) Nominal costs of borrowing will always be low.
(C) Business activity will tend to increase.
(D) Investment will be encouraged.

(2 marks)

Question 57

Which ONE of the following would cause the value of the multiplier to fall?

(A) A fall in the level of government expenditure.
(B) A rise in the marginal propensity to consume.
(C) A fall in business investment.
(D) A rise in the marginal propensity to save.

(2 marks)

Question 58

The recession phase of the trade cycle will normally be accompanied by all of the following EXCEPT which ONE?

(A) A rise in the rate of inflation.
(B) A fall in the level of national output.
(C) An improvement in the trade balance.
(D) A rise in the level of unemployment.

(2 marks)

Question 59

According to the new classical school, in order to manage the economy governments should:

(A) use active fiscal and monetary policy.
(B) adopt a laissez faire approach and leave everything to market forces.
(C) announce monetary rules to control inflation, and liberalise product and factor markets.
(D) use only monetary policy to increase output and employment.

(2 marks)

Question 60

The following is a list of types of unemployment.

Structural unemployment
Cyclical unemployment
Real wage (classical) unemployment
Frictional unemployment.
Seasonal unemployment

Match the above types of unemployment to the following definitions.

Definition of unemployment	Type of unemployment
(i) Unemployment that occurs in particular industries and arises from long-term changes in the patterns of demand and supply.	
(ii) Unemployment associated with industries or regions where the demand for labour and wage rates regularly rise and fall over the year.	

(2 marks)

Question 61

All of the following will lead to a fall in the level of economic activity in an economy EXCEPT which ONE?

(A) A rise in cyclical unemployment.
(B) A fall in business investment.
(C) A decrease in government expenditure.
(D) A rise in interest rates.

(2 marks)

? Question 62

The best measure of the standard of living in a country is

(A) gross domestic product per capita.
(B) per capita personal consumption.
(C) gross national product per capita.
(D) personal disposable income.

(2 marks)

? Question 63

Supply side policy is designed to

(A) raise the level of aggregate monetary demand in the economy.
(B) manage the money supply in the economy.
(C) improve the ability of the economy to produce goods and services.
(D) reduce unemployment by limiting the supply of labour.

(2 marks)

? Question 64

Indicate whether each of the following taxes are direct taxes or indirect taxes.

Type of tax	Direct	Indirect
Income tax		
Value added tax		
Corporation tax		
National insurance (social security tax)		

(4 marks)

? Question 65

International trade is best explained by the fact that:

(A) all countries have an absolute advantage in the production of something.
(B) all countries have specialised in the production of certain goods and services.
(C) no country has an absolute advantage in the production of all goods and services.
(D) all countries have a comparative advantage in the production of something.

(2 marks)

Question 66

The following diagram shows the aggregate demand curve (AD) and the aggregate supply curve (AS) for an economy:

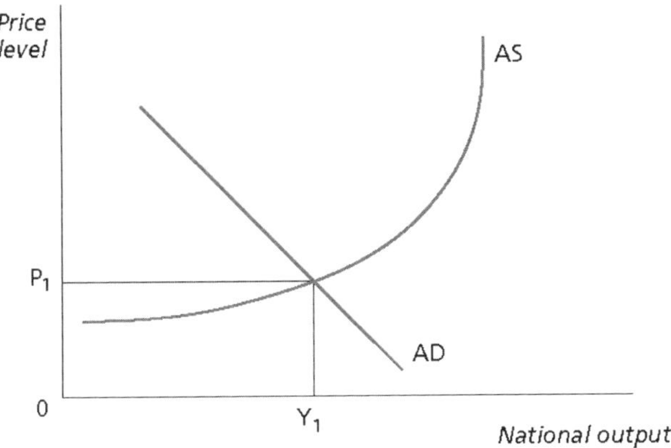

With reference to the diagram:
A .... supply shock would shift the .... curve to the left and cause the rate of inflation to increase. However the level of .... would fall. A(n) .... fiscal policy would shift the .... curve to the right leading to a .... in both the level of national output and the rate of inflation.

Use the following words and phrases to fill in the gaps in the above passage.

positive
aggregate demand
rise
expansionary
negative
deflationary
aggregate supply
inflation
national output
fall

(6 marks)

Question 67

All of the following will encourage the process of the globalisation of production EXCEPT which ONE?

(A) Reductions in international transport costs.
(B) Higher levels of tariffs.
(C) Reduced barriers to international capital movements.
(D) Increased similarity in demand patterns between countries.

(2 marks)

Question 68

Intra-industry trade occurs when a country:

(A) exports and imports different products.
(B) exports and imports the same products.
(C) imports materials to be used by its domestic industry.
(D) exports materials for use in industries in other countries.

(2 marks)

Question 69

Which ONE of the following shows the lowest degree of international mobility?

(A) Unskilled labour.
(B) Financial capital.
(C) Technical knowledge.
(D) Management.

(2 marks)

Question 70

Identify which of the following statements about the balance of payments is true and which is false.

Statement	True	False
(i) A deficit on a country's balance of payments current account can be financed by a surplus of invisible earnings.		
(ii) Flows of profits and interest on capital appear in the Capital Account.		
(iii) Flexible exchange rate systems should, in principle, prevent persistent current account imbalances.		
(iv) Current account deficits tend to worsen in periods of rapid economic growth.		

(4 marks)

Question 71

A fall in the exchange rate for a country's currency will improve the balance of payments current account if:

(A) the price elasticity of demand for imports is greater than for exports.
(B) the price elasticity of demand for exports is greater than for imports.
(C) the sum of the price elasticities for imports and exports is less than one.
(D) the sum of the price elasticities for imports and exports is greater than one.

(2 marks)

Question 72

All of the following are benefits which all countries gain when adopting a single currency such as the Euro, EXCEPT which ONE?

(A) Reduced transactions costs.
(B) Increased price transparency.
(C) Lower interest rates.
(D) Reduced exchange rate uncertainty.

(2 marks)

Question 73

For each of the following events, indicate whether the direct effect of each on an economy would raise inflation, reduce inflation or leave the rate of inflation unaffected. Assume that the economy is close to full employment.

Event	Raise inflation	Lower inflation	Leave inflation unchanged
(i) A rise (appreciation) in the exchange for the country's currency.			
(ii) A significant increase in the money supply.			
(iii) The removal of house prices from the consumer price index.			
(iv) A rise in business expectations leading to an increase in investment.			

(4 marks)

Question 74

Compared to a fixed exchange rate system, an economy will benefit from a flexible exchange rate system because:

(A) it enables businesses to vary their export prices.
(B) governments will not have to deflate the economy when balance of payments deficits occur.
(C) it reduces the cost of acquiring foreign exchange.
(D) it ensures that businesses never become uncompetitive in international markets.

(2 marks)

? Question 75

All of the following statements are true EXCEPT which ONE?

(A) Import quotas tend to reduce prices.
(B) Trade protection tends to reduce consumer choice.
(C) Trade protection tends to reduce exports.
(D) Tariffs tend to reduce competition.

(2 marks)

Mock Assessment – Solutions

Solution 1

A

Solution 2

C

Solution 3

10%

Solution 4

C

Solution 5

(a) $25
(b) $14
(c) 12 or 13
(d) 12

Solution 6

B

Solution 7

(a) $6716
(b) No
(c) $7076

Solution 8

B

Solution 9

C

Solution 10

The *stakeholders* in a company are all those who have an interest in the strategy and behaviour of the *company*. Their interest may not always coincide with those of the *shareholders* who are principally interested in *profits*. The task of *management* is to attempt to reconcile these conflicting interests.

Solution 11

Statement		True	False
(i)	Shareholders are not liable for the debts of the company.	X	
(ii)	Owners always exercise day-to-day decision making authority.		X
(iii)	Owners share in the profits of the company, but not necessarily in proportion to the number of shares that they own.		X

Solution 12

B

Solution 13

Economic process	Raise curve	Lower curve	Leave curve unaffected
A rise in wage costs.	X		
Increase opportunities for economies of scale.			X
A fall in the price of raw materials.		X	
A shift in the demand curve to the left.			X

Solution 14

Statement	True	False
The law of diminishing returns shows how long run cost tends to rise if the scale of output becomes too great		X
A firm's short run cost curve is always U shaped; the long cost curve may or may not be	X	
For most firms technological change is one of the most important economies of scale		X
Economies of scale act as barrier to entry to industries.	X	

Solution 15

Characteristic	Yes	No
A large number of small firms.		X
A preference for non-price competition over price competition	X	
Interdependence of decision making	X	
Ease of entry and exit to and from the industry		X

Solution 16

Statement	True	False
Collusion is more likely in oligopoly markets than in other markets	X	
If there are economies of scale, a monopoly firm may charge lower prices than equivalent firms facing competition	X	
Oligopolistic firms can never achieve lower long run costs than could competitive firms in the same industry		X
Oligopolistic firms can make excess profits but only in the short run.		X

Solution 17

B

Solution 18

D

Solution 19

A

Solution 20

Company		Sales	Market Share (in %)
No 1		1200	24
No 2		800	16
No 3		600	12
No 4		600	12
No 5		500	10
No 6		500	10
No 7		450	9
No 8		350	7
The four-firm concentration ratio	64%		

Solution 21

B

Solution 22

A

Solution 23

B

Solution 24

A

Solution 25

D

Solution 26

(a) (i) Externalities
(b) (iii) Public goods and services
(c) (v) Monopsony power
(d) (ii) Monopoly power

Solution 27

D

Solution 28

(a) (i) Horizontal merger
(b) (ii) Vertical merger
(c) (i) Horizontal merger
(d) (iii) Conglomerate merger

Solution 29

Statement	True	False
(i) Privatisation increases the commercial pressure on the business to make a profit.	X	
(ii) Privatisation ensures the business faces competition and so encourages greater efficiency.		X
(iii) Privatisation is a means of solving the principal–agent problem.		X
(iv) Privatisation is likely to make the business more responsive to needs of its customers.	X	

Solution 30

C

Solution 31

B

Solution 32

(a) Below the optimum output.
(b) At the profit maximising level.
(c) Area PC – Q1

Solution 33

A

Solution 34

C

Solution 35

C

Solution 36

C

Solution 37

A

Solution 38

C

Solution 39

A

Solution 40

Situation	Market Structure
(i) In the long run, abnormal profits are competed away by the entry of new firms and for each firm output will be the optimum level of output.	*Perfect competition*
(ii) The behaviour of any one firm is conditioned by how it expects its competitors to react to its price and output decisions.	*Oligopoly*

Solution 41

D

Solution 42

B

Solution 43

D

Solution 44

B

Solution 45

Instrument	Asset	Liability
Advances	X	
Money at call with discount houses	X	
Deposit accounts		X
Shareholder capital.		X

Solution 46

B

Solution 47

C

Solution 48

B

Solution 49

A business will need to insure itself against a range of risks. It can do so by employing a *broker* to seek out the most appropriate insurance policies. If the risks involved are very large the insurance company *underwriting* the risk may engage in *reinsuring* the risk with other companies.

Solution 50

A

Solution 51

Statement	Supply	Demand
Payments for imports into the country.	X	
Inflows of capital into the country.		X
Purchases of foreign currency by the country's central bank.	X	

Solution 52

D

Solution 53

B

Solution 54

D

Solution 55

A

Solution 56

B

Solution 57

D

Solution 58

A

Solution 59

C

Solution 60

Definition of unemployment	Type of unemployment
(i) Unemployment that occurs in particular industries and arises from long-term changes in the patterns of demand and supply.	*Structural unemployment*
(ii) Unemployment associated with industries or regions where the demand for labour and wage rates regularly rise and fall over the year.	*Seasonal unemployment*

Solution 61

A

Solution 62

B

Solution 63

C

Solution 64

Type of tax	Direct	Indirect
Income tax	X	
Value added tax		X
Corporation tax	X	
National insurance (social security tax)	X	

Solution 65

D

Solution 66

A *negative* supply shock would shift the *aggregate supply* curve to the left and cause the rate of inflation to increase. However the level of *national output* would fall. An *expansionary*. fiscal policy would shift the *aggregate demand* curve to the right leading to a *rise* in both the level of national output and the rate of inflation.

✓ Solution 67

B

✓ Solution 68

B

✓ Solution 69

A

✓ Solution 70

Statement	True	False
(i) A deficit on a country's balance of payments current account can be financed by a surplus of invisible earnings.		X
(ii) Flows of profits and interest on capital appear in the Capital Account.		X
(iii) Flexible exchange rate systems should, in principle, prevent persistent current account imbalances.	X	
(iv) Current account deficits tend to worsen in periods of rapid economic growth.	X	

✓ Solution 71

D

✓ Solution 72

C

✓ Solution 73

Event	Raise inflation	Lower inflation	Leave inflation unchanged
(i) A rise (appreciation) in the exchange for the country's currency.		X	
(ii) A significant increase in the money supply.	X		
(iii) The removal of house prices from the consumer price index.			X
(iv) A rise in business expectations leading to an increase in investment.	X		

✓ Solution 74

B

✓ Solution 75

A

Mock Assessment 2

Paper C04
Fundamentals of Business Economics

Instructions: attempt all 75 questions

Time allowed 2 hours

Do not turn the page until you are ready to attempt the assessment under timed conditions

Mock Assessment – Questions

Question 1

There has been a fall in the prices of raw materials that are used as inputs by all producers of a manufactured product that is sold in a perfectly competitive market for the finished product. Demand conditions for the final product are unchanged, and the demand curve has the normal negative slope. The effect of this change on the market price and quantity bought and sold of the final product will be:

(A) A higher price and higher quantity.
(B) A lower price and lower quantity.
(C) A lower price and higher quantity.
(D) A higher price and lower quantity.

(2 marks)

Question 2

You observe that the price of a product has risen by 10% and its sales have fallen by 10%. Which one of the following on its own could have caused this?

(A) The demand curve has an elasticity greater (in absolute size) than –1.
(B) A technical advance has shifted the supply curve to the right and demand elasticity is close to –1.
(C) The price of a substitute has fallen and supply elasticity is close to 1.
(D) Wages paid by suppliers have risen so the supply curve has shifted to the left and demand elasticity is close to –1.

(2 marks)

Question 3

The price of a product falls from £100 to £99 and the quantity demanded rises from 1,000 to 1,100. Which one of the following is a true statement about the value of demand elasticity (as measured at the initial price and quantity)?

(A) Elasticity is –10.
(B) Elasticity is –0.1.
(C) Elasticity is –1.
(D) Elasticity is +100.

(2 marks)

Question 4

Theatre attendances fell last year even though prices of admission also fell. Which one of the following on its own could explain this?

(A) There was an increase in the supply of theatre seats but no change affecting demand conditions.
(B) There was an increased demand from consumers for visits to the theatre as the quality of TV deteriorated.

(C) There was a reduction in prices of cinema seats as many new multiplex cinemas opened up.
(D) There was an increase in the cost of putting on plays.

(2 marks)

Question 5

The equilibrium for each firm in a perfectly competitive industry in the long run (that is where there is no further incentive for entry or exit of firms) will be characterised by which of the following?

(A) It sets MC = MR; price exceeds average total cost, and it makes positive economic profit (also known as abnormal or excess profit).
(B) It sets MC = price; average variable cost is at its minimum; and price exceeds average total cost.
(C) It sets MC = MR; it produces at the minimum point of average total cost curve and makes zero economic profit.
(D) It sets MC = MR; MC cuts MR from above; and price exceeds average fixed cost.

(2 marks)

Question 6

A profit maximising monopolist will:

(A) Set price equal to marginal cost.
(B) Set price equal to average variable cost.
(C) Set marginal cost equal to marginal revenue and produce at the point of minimum average total cost.
(D) Choose the output for which marginal cost equals marginal revenue and set a price above marginal cost.

(2 marks)

Question 7

In monopolistic competition, which one of the following is true?

(A) The outcome is the same as in pure monopoly in the short run and the same as perfect competition in the long run.
(B) Each producer faces a downward sloping demand curve, sets MC = MR and makes no profit in the long run.
(C) Each producer sets marginal cost equal to price in both the short run and the long run.
(D) Each producer sets MC equal to price in the long run but not in the short run.

(2 marks)

Question 8

Below are five possible statements about rules for profit maximisation for any firm in the short run.

(i) Marginal cost must be equal to marginal revenue.
(ii) The marginal cost must be rising relative to marginal revenue at the optimum.
(iii) The marginal revenue must be rising relative to marginal cost at the optimum.

(iv) The product price must exceed average variable cost for some range of production.
(v) Average fixed cost must be at its minimum point.

Which one combination of these conditions is correct?

(A) (i), (iv) and (v).
(B) (i), (ii) and (iv).
(C) (ii), (iii) and (iv).
(D) (iii), (iv) and (v).

(2 marks)

Question 9

The demand curve for a specific input for a profit maximising firm will be the same as:

(A) The demand curve for the final product.
(B) The downward sloping part of the average product curve of the input.
(C) The downward sloping part of the marginal revenue product curve of the input.
(D) The marginal cost curve of the input.

(2 marks)

Question 10

Which of the following is NOT a source of market failure:

(A) Externalities.
(B) Common property resources.
(C) Asymmetric information.
(D) Constant returns to scale.

(2 marks)

Question 11

There has been a fall in input prices for all producers of a good sold in a competitive industry. Assuming this is a normal good, the effect of this change on market price and quantity will be (choose only one).

(A) A higher price and higher quantity.
(B) A lower price and lower quantity.
(C) A lower price and higher quantity.
(D) A higher price and lower quantity.

(2 marks)

Question 12

The price of a product rises from £20 to £22 and the quantity demanded falls from 10,000 to 9,000. Which one of the following is a true statement about the value of demand elasticity (as measured at the initial price and quantity)?

(A) Elasticity is –0.1.
(B) Elasticity is –1.
(C) Elasticity is –0.5.
(D) Elasticity is –2.

(2 marks)

Question 13

A firm can sell its product for £40 each in a competitive output market, its total cost of production for the production range of 400 units to 405 units is given below:

400	401	402	403	404
£12,600	£12,630	£12,665	£12,730	£12,900

What is the profit maximising level of production?

(A) 401
(B) 402
(C) 403
(D) 404

(2 marks)

Question 14

In monopolistic competition, which one of the following is true?

(A) MC = MR
(B) MR = 0
(C) MC = Price
(D) AC = MC

(2 marks)

Question 15

The price of coffee beans rose by 5% last year and quantity purchased rose by 5%.

(A) There was an increase in supply as a result of new production techniques but not changes in conditions of demand.
(B) Consumer incomes increased substantially and coffee is a normal good.
(C) The price of cocoa fell substantially and cocoa is a substitute for coffee.
(D) There was a major frost in Brazil that reduced its coffee production, and Brazil has a big share of world production.

(2 marks)

Question 16

Brand X sold 500,000 items at £200 each last year. It is known that its price elasticity of demand is –0.5 (calculated at the current price and quantity). What would sales be this year if there are no other changes affecting demand and the price per unit is raised to £220?

(A) 475,000
(B) 400,000
(C) 450,000
(D) 525,000

(2 marks)

Question 17

A firm can sell its product for £25 each in a competitive output market. Its total cost of production for the production range of 200 units to 205 units is given below:

200	201	202	203	204	205
£3,600	£3,615	£3,634	£3,658	£3,688	£3,720

What is the profit maximising level of production?

(A) 201
(B) 202
(C) 203
(D) 204

(2 marks)

Question 18

A profit maximising firm which has a given capital stock has to decide how many workers to hire per week in the range of 10–15. The weekly wage that has to be paid to every worker is constant at £450 and the total revenue per week received after hiring the numbers of possible workers is given below:

Workers	10	11	12	13	14	15
Total revenue	£10,500	£11,200	£11,750	£12,205	£12,400	£12,750

How many workers will be hired?

(A) 11
(B) 15
(C) 14
(D) 13

(2 marks)

Question 19

Which of the following is NOT a source of market failure?

(A) Public goods.
(B) Common property resources.
(C) Inefficient exclusion.
(D) Diminishing returns to scale.

(2 marks)

Question 20

A scarce resource is one for which:

(A) Opportunity cost is high.
(B) The demand at zero price would exceed supply.
(C) Demand always exceeds supply.
(D) There is a finite supply.

(2 marks)

Question 21

The price elasticity of demand for an inferior good:

(A) Must be positive.
(B) Must be negative.
(C) Must be zero.
(D) Could be any of the above.

(2 marks)

Question 22

Prices are most volatile when:

(A) Supply is elastic, demand is elastic.
(B) Supply is inelastic, demand is inelastic.
(C) Supply is elastic, demand is inelastic.
(D) Supply is inelastic, demand is elastic.

(2 marks)

Question 23

What do economists mean by the term opportunity cost?

(A) The value of the best alternative use for a resource.
(B) The price equilibrium of the scarce good.
(C) The cost of allocating scarce resources.
(D) None of the above.

(2 marks)

Question 24

The income elasticity of demand for a luxury good is:

(A) Positive.
(B) Negative.
(C) Zero.
(D) Any of the above.

(2 marks)

Question 25

Which of the following events would shift the demand curve for Good A to the left?

(A) An increase in the price of Good X.
(B) An increase in the price of a substitute good.
(C) An increase in the price of a complementary good.
(D) An increase in consumer income.

(2 marks)

? Question 26

Which one of the following will shift the supply curve for Good B to the right?

(A) An increase in the subsidy paid to produce Good B.
(B) A reduction in labour productivity while producing Good B.
(C) An increase in the price of raw materials used to produce Good B.
(D) An increase in wages paid to workers who produce Good B.

(2 marks)

? Question 27

A minimum price is set for Good X at £100 which is below the free market price. A decrease in the supply of Good X, keeping the minimum price fixed at £100 will result in:

(A) A rise in price and a surplus of Good X.
(B) A rise in price and a shortage of Good X.
(C) A rise in price and a balance between supply and demand for Good X.
(D) No change in price and a shortage of Good X.

(2 marks)

? Question 28

If the income elasticity of demand for Good X is 2, a rise in consumer income from £500 to £520 will increase the quantity demanded of Good X by:

(A) 2%
(B) 4%
(C) 6%
(D) 8%

(2 marks)

? Question 29

Which one of the following is not a feature of a free market?

(A) Demand.
(B) Supply.
(C) Prices.
(D) Government intervention.

(2 marks)

? Question 30

A car manufacturer acquiring a car dealership is an example of:

(A) Horizontal integration – forward.
(B) Horizontal integration – backwards.
(C) Vertical integration – forward.
(D) Vertical integration – backwards.

(2 marks)

Question 31

Which of the following is a natural barrier to entry?

(A) High entry cost
(B) Patent.
(C) Government regulation.
(D) Nationalisation.

(2 marks)

Question 32

Which of the following is not associated with perfect competition?

(A) Homogeneous products.
(B) Marginal cost = price.
(C) Marginal cost = marginal revenue.
(D) Barriers to entry.

(2 marks)

Question 33

Which of the following is associated with monopolistic competition?

(A) Barriers to entry.
(B) Economies of scale.
(C) Excess capacity.
(D) None of the above.

(2 marks)

Question 34

To belong to a cartel in the model of oligopoly, firms have got to 'abide by the rules'. These rules are:

(A) To stick to the price and the output that is set by the cartel.
(B) To stick to the price but not the output that is set by the cartel.
(C) To stick to the output but not the price that is set by the cartel.
(D) There are no formal rules when joining a cartel.

(2 marks)

Question 35

The expenditure method of measuring national income:

(A) Measures economic activity by summing the value of expenditure on consumer goods.
(B) Measures economic activity by summing of expenditure on final goods.
(C) Measures economic activity by summing the value of expenditure on all goods.
(D) Is determined by the income method.

(2 marks)

Question 36

Net national product is equal to:

(A) GDP less net property income from abroad less depreciation.
(B) GDP plus net property income from abroad.
(C) GDP less depreciation.
(D) GDP plus net property income from abroad less depreciation.

(2 marks)

Question 37

Suppose that in a closed economy, consumption expenditure is equal to 80% of disposable income. If the government were to reduce both its spending and taxation by £100 million, what would be the impact on equilibrium national income?

(A) Nothing.
(B) National income would rise by £100m.
(C) National income would fall by £100m.
(D) Impossible to determine without further details.

(2 marks)

Question 38

A world recession is likely to lead to:

(A) A leftward shift in a country's macroeconomic demand schedule.
(B) A rightward shift in a country's short-run aggregate supply curve.
(C) A rightward shift in a country's macroeconomic demand schedule.
(D) A leftward shift in a country's short-run aggregate supply curve.

(2 marks)

Question 39

Consider the following data for country Y:

Year 20X8	NI	£500m	PI 100
Year 20X9	NI	£600m	PI 120

where NI = national income and where PI = price index.

In real terms, the economy between 20X8 and 20X9:

(A) Rose by £100 million.
(B) Rose by £120 million.
(C) Fell by £20 million.
(D) Remained the same.

(2 marks)

Question 40

An economy is made up of three firms. Firm A mines a raw material, it pays £200 to its workers and it sells £200 worth of output to firm B and £300 worth to firm C (it has no other sales or costs). Firm B makes a consumer good and sells £400 worth, paying £200 to its workers. Firm C also makes a consumer good, selling £600 worth and paying its workers £200. There are no transactions between firms B and C. What is the value of GDP?

(A) £1,200
(B) £800
(C) £1,000
(D) £700

(2 marks)

Question 41

The short-run aggregate supply curve is positively sloped because:

(A) Input prices rise as output expands.
(B) With given input prices, firms' unit costs rise with output.
(C) Firms are faced with increasing returns to scale.
(D) Input prices rise when there is an inflationary gap.

(2 marks)

Question 42

If the economy starts at potential GDP, has a positively sloped short run aggregate supply curve, and there is an exogenous increase in export demand, the effects will be:

(A) In the short run, output will rise while prices fall and in the long run prices will return to the original position and GDP will be higher.
(B) In the short run, there will be some increase in GDP and some in prices, but in the long-run there will be higher prices but no increase in GDP.
(C) In the short run, there will be some fall in GDP and prices, but both will return to their starting point in the long run.
(D) In the short run, prices will rise while GDP falls, and both will return to their initial position in the long run.

(2 marks)

Question 43

Which of the following statements about the balance of payments is NOT correct?

(A) Payments that lead to demands for foreign currency are measured as debits, while payments that lead to supplies of foreign exchange are measured as credits.
(B) The current account balance plus the capital and financial account balances add up to zero.
(C) A current account deficit is a sign of a weak economy, while a current account surplus is a sign of a strong economy.
(D) A current account surplus implies that domestic residents are increasing their net foreign assets.

(2 marks)

Question 44

The government is concerned about the high level of voluntary unemployment within the economy. Which of the following policies would be most appropriate to deal with this problem?

(A) Reduce minimum wages.
(B) Increase unemployment benefit.
(C) Reduce the level of taxes on income.
(D) Reduce the level of taxes on expenditure.

(2 marks)

Question 45

The aggregate demand curve is negatively sloped because:

(A) Firms will only produce more at higher prices.
(B) Input prices rise as output increases.
(C) Tax revenue rises at higher prices.
(D) Consumer spending falls at higher price levels owing to the fall in real value of their savings, and net exports fall as domestic goods' prices rise relative to foreign prices.

(2 marks)

Question 46

An economy is made up of three firms. Firm A mines a raw material, it pays £200 to its workers and it sells £600 worth of output to firm B and £800 worth to firm C (it has no other sales or costs). Firm B makes a consumer good and sells £1,400 worth, paying £400 to its workers. Firm C also makes a consumer good, selling £2,200 worth and paying its workers £800. There are no transactions between firms B and C, and there are no taxes or government spending, and no imports and exports. What is the value of GDP?

(A) £2,400
(B) £3,600
(C) £2,000
(D) £2,300

(2 marks)

Question 47

Which of the following must always balance?

(A) Visible balance.
(B) Invisible balance.
(C) Capital account.
(D) The balance of payments.

(2 marks)

Question 48

Which of the following explains why countries may benefit from international trade, according to the principle of comparative advantage?

(A) By specialising in production of goods, which can be made relatively cheaply, and trading with others who specialise in producing different products, all can become better off.

(B) Trade involves domestic jobs moving to countries that have cheaper labour, and this means that the country with high priced labour is worse off as a result.
(C) Specialisation and trade only works under the protection of tariffs.
(D) Nations can only benefit from international trade if some other country loses.

(2 marks)

Question 49

Final goods are:

(A) Goods that will finally be used up to produce other goods.
(B) Goods which cannot be improved in the short run.
(C) Goods which are purchased by the ultimate user.
(D) None of the above.

(2 marks)

Question 50

The average propensity to consume may be defined as:

(A) Change in consumption divided by the change in disposable income.
(B) Level of consumption divided by the level of disposable income.
(C) Level of consumption divided by the change in disposable income.
(D) Change in consumption divided by the level of disposable income.

(2 marks)

Question 51

Which of the following items would be counted as part of national income?

(i) Child allowance.
(ii) A housekeeper's salary.
(iii) The pay of a fire officer.

(A) (i) and (ii).
(B) (ii) and (iii).
(C) (i) only.
(D) (ii) only.

(2 marks)

Question 52

The accelerator principle states that:

(A) Investment is increased when interest rates fall.
(B) An increase in consumer demand leads to a more than proportionate increase in the level of investment.
(C) An increase in investment will lead to a more than proportionate increase in output.
(D) The rate of change of investment affects the rate of change of output

(2 marks)

Question 53

Household saving is equal to:

(A) Disposable income less taxes and consumption expenditure.
(B) Disposable income less imports, taxes and consumption expenditure.
(C) Disposable income less imports and consumption expenditure.
(D) Disposable income less consumption expenditure.

(2 marks)

Question 54

If in a closed economy, consumption expenditure increases from £18,000 to £19,500 when national income increases from £20,000 to £26,000, then the marginal propensity to consume out of national income is:

(A) 0.25 and the multiplier is 1.33.
(B) 0.75 and the multiplier is 1.33.
(C) 0.25 and the multiplier is 2.
(D) 0.75 and the multiplier is 2.

(2 marks)

Question 55

A fall in real gross domestic product would result from an increase in all of the following except:

(A) Savings.
(B) Imports.
(C) Taxation.
(D) Government expenditure.

(2 marks)

Question 56

The difference in the shape of the short-run and the long-run aggregate supply curve can be explained by the assumption that:

(A) Capital is fixed in the short run but variable in the long run.
(B) Money illusion exists in the short run but not in the long run.
(C) The Central Bank can control the supply of money in the long run.
(D) Wage constraints are fixed in the long run.

(2 marks)

Question 57

The residual error is to be found in the:

(i) Output method.
(ii) Expenditure method.
(iii) Income method.

(A) (i) and (ii).
(B) (i) and (iii).
(C) (ii) and (iii).
(D) (i), (ii) and (iii).

(2 marks)

Question 58

According to Keynes:

(A) Both transactions and speculative demand for money are a function of income.
(B) Both transactions and speculative demand for money are a function of interest rates.
(C) Transactions demand is a function of income, speculative demand is a function of interest rates.
(D) Transactions demand is a function of interest rates, speculative demand is a function of income.

(2 marks)

Question 59

Which of the following is NOT an example of short-term finance?

(A) Bank overdraft.
(B) Trade credit.
(C) Venture capital.
(D) Factoring.

(2 marks)

Question 60

Which of the following financial institutions would be associated with the money market?

(i) Banks.
(ii) Discount houses.
(iii) Investment trusts.
(iv) Unit trusts.

(A) (i) and (ii).
(B) (i) and (iii).
(C) (ii) and (iii).
(D) (ii) and (iv).

(2 marks)

Question 61

Someone who sells shares because they believe that the price is about to fall is known as a:

(A) Bull.
(B) Bear.
(C) Stag.
(D) Horse.

(2 marks)

Question 62

If a discount house offered the Central Bank £95 for a £100 short-term (90 days) gilt, the approximate annual rate of return would be:

(A) 5%
(B) 10%
(C) 15%
(D) 21%

(2 marks)

Question 63

If the government were frightened that the economy is going to enter a recession, the best course of action would be:

(A) Raise interest rates, raise the reserve asset ratio.
(B) Lower interest rates, lower the reserve asset ratio.
(C) Raise interest rates, lower the reserve asset ratio.
(D) Lower interest rates, raise the reserve asset ratio.

(2 marks)

Question 64

The purchasing power parity path is:

(A) The path that economists think that a currency will always follow.
(B) The path that the domestic money supply must follow to keep prices at the world level.
(C) The path of the real exchange rate that would keep the nominal exchange rate constant.
(D) The path of the nominal exchange rate that would keep the real exchange rate constant.

(2 marks)

Question 65

A sudden discrete fall in the fixed exchange rate which the government commits itself to defend is called a:

(A) Revaluation.
(B) Appreciation.
(C) Devaluation.
(D) Depreciation.

(2 marks)

? Question 66

Country A exports Good X to Country B and imports Good Y from Country B. If the price of X rises by 40% and the price of Y falls by 30%, what can be said about Country A's terms of trade?

(A) They have improved by 40%.
(B) They have improved by 70%.
(C) They have improved by 100%.
(D) They have deteriorated by 100%.

(2 marks)

? Question 67

Assuming a floating exchange rate system in the USA, if the level of US short-term interest rates falls, the exchange rate of the dollar will:

(A) Rise and stay at its new higher level.
(B) Rise in the short term and then fall back close to its previous level.
(C) Fall and stay at its new lower level.
(D) Fall in the short term and then rise back close to its previous level.

(2 marks)

? Question 68

Which of the following best characterises the views of a monetarist?

(A) In the long term, unemployment can be reduced by an expansionary fiscal policy.
(B) In the long term, unemployment can be reduced by an expansionary monetary policy.
(C) In the long term, unemployment can be reduced by increasing efficiency and productivity.
(D) In the long term, unemployment can be reduced but only at the cost of a higher rate of inflation.

(2 marks)

? Question 69

In Country C it takes ten hours of labour to make one unit of Good U and five hours to make one unit of Good V. In Country D it takes six hours of labour to make one unit of U and nine hours to make one unit of V. Which of the following statements is correct?

(A) Country C has a comparative advantage in the production of both Good U and Good V.
(B) Country D has an absolute advantage in the production of Good U and Country C has a comparative advantage in the production of Good V.
(C) Country C has a comparative advantage in the production of Good V and an absolute advantage in the production of Good U.
(D) Country D has an absolute advantage in the production of both Good U and Good V.

(2 marks)

Question 70

If the UK's current account balance is in deficit by £7bn, its capital account in surplus by £4bn, and sales of foreign exchange reserves amount to £2bn:

(A) The UK can repay £1bn of IMF loans.
(B) The UK needs additional IMF loans of £1bn.
(C) The UK can repay £5bn of IMF loans.
(D) The UK needs additional IMF loans of £5bn.

(2 marks)

Question 71

The advantages of fixed exchange rates include:

(i) Monetary policy is more effective.
(ii) There will be no need to hold gold reserves.
(iii) Fiscal policy is more effective.

(A) (i) and (ii).
(B) (ii) and (iii).
(C) (i) only.
(D) (iii) only.

(2 marks)

Question 72

If a country's terms of trade index falls, this means that:

(i) Export prices have risen faster than import prices.
(ii) The country needs to sell foreign exchange reserves.
(iii) Import prices have risen faster than export prices.

(A) (i) and (ii).
(B) (ii) and (iii).
(C) (i) only.
(D) (iii) only.

(2 marks)

Question 73

An increase in the value of the pound sterling will:

(i) Worsen the UK's terms of trade.
(ii) Improve the UK's balance of trade.
(iii) Improve the UK's terms of trade.

(A) (i) and (ii).
(B) (ii) and (iii).
(C) (i) only.
(D) (iii) only.

(2 marks)

? Question 74

If the U.K.'s deficit on current account is in deficit by £17bn, its capital account in surplus by £8bn, and sales of foreign exchange reserves are £2bn, which of the following statements is true?

(A) The U.K. can repay £7bn of IMF loans
(B) The U.K. requires a further £7bn in IMF loans
(C) The U.K. can repay £11bn of IMF loans
(D) The U.K. requires a further £11bn in IMF loans

(2 marks)

? Question 75

Which one of the following satisfies the Marshall – Lerner condition?

(A) Demand for exports is elastic
(B) Demand for imports is inelastic
(C) The sum of the price elasticities of demand for exports and imports must be greater than 1
(D) None of the above

(2 marks)

Mock Assessment – Answers

Solution 1

If there has been a fall in the price of raw materials, this should result in a fall in price, which will lead to more being purchased.

So C.

Solution 2

If price has risen by 10%, this indicates a shift to the left in the supply curve and if demand has also fallen by 10%, this indicates that price elasticity of demand is near –1.

So D

Solution 3

Change in demand +100
Change in price −1

% Change +10
% Change −1
So −10.

Answer A.

Solution 4

Reduction in price can be explained by increase in supply, so A or C. Alternative A states that demand stays the same, so by process of elimination answer must be C.

Solution 5

Equilibrium:

(i) MC = MR.
(ii) AC minimised.
(iii) Makes zero economic profit.

So C.

Solution 6

At a price above where MC = MR.

So D.

Solution 7

(i) Each producer faces downward sloping demand curve.
(ii) Set price where MC = MR.
(iii) No profit in the long run.

So B.

Solution 8

(i) Marginal cost equals marginal revenue.
(ii) Marginal cost must be rising relative to marginal revenue.
(iv) The product price must exceed average variable cost for some range of production.

So alternative B.

Solution 9

The demand curve for a specific input for a profit maximising firm will be the same as the downward sloping part of the marginal revenue product curve of the input.

So C.

Solution 10

Constant returns to scale are often a feature of a market or industry but they are not a source of market failure in the way of, say monopoly power.

So D.

Solution 11

This is very similar to question 1, using the same rationale.

Answer C.

Solution 12

Demand	% Fall	−10%
Price	% Rise	+10%

Answer −1, so B.

Solution 13

Two methods can be used here. We can work out total revenue at each output and subtract total cost at each output, but this is time consuming.

Alternatively, profit will rise if MR exceeds MC. This continues up until 402, but once we reach 403 MC > MR.

So answer is B.

Solution 14

Answer A.

Firms attempt to maximise profits where MC = MR. All other statements are false.

Solution 15

The only possible answer here is that consumer incomes increased substantially and coffee is a normal good.

So B.

Solution 16

If price is raised from £200 to £220, this is a 10% price increase.

If elasticity of demand is –0.5, then there has been a 5% reduction in demand. 5% of 500,000 is equal to 25,000.

So answer is A – 475,000.

Solution 17

Similar question to 13. Again, using marginal cost and marginal revenue profit maximising output is 203. At 204 MC = £30 but MR is only £25.

So C.

Solution 18

Again similar to previous question, except this time we are calculating marginal revenue product, i.e. revenue generated by hiring one more worker. As long as revenue generated exceeds £450, we continue to hire up until 13. If we took on the 14th worker our MR is only £195, so we stop at 13.

Answer D.

Solution 19

Similar to question 10. Diminishing returns is a feature of many industries but is not an example of market failure.

So D.

Solution 20

Non-economists might have gone for alternative D, but B is technically the correct answer.

So B.

Solution 21

An inferior good is one where quantity demanded falls as income rises. It has nothing to do with price, so price elasticity of demand could have any value.

So D.

Solution 22

On a question like this, draw a diagram on a scrap piece of paper. Where demand and supply are inelastic, adjustment comes on price. Where they are elastic, adjustment comes on quantity. So volatility will occur when they are both inelastic.

So B.

Solution 23

Only one answer here, the value of the best alternative use for a resource.

So A.

Solution 24

Not only will it be positive, it will also be greater than 1.

So A.

Solution 25

A leftward shift in the demand curve represents a fall in demand so, if the price of a complementary good increases, then the demand for that good will decrease.

So C.

Solution 26

A shift to the right in a supply curve indicates an increase in supply which could only be caused by an increase in the subsidy paid to produce the good.

So A.

Solution 27

Setting the minimum price below the original free market equilibrium price has no effect on the original equilibrium, so price is determined by supply and demand.

A decrease in supply will shift supply to the left. This will increase equilibrium price and reduce equilibrium quantity, therefore there will be a balance between supply and demand.

So C.

Solution 28

If price rises from £500 to £520, this is a 4% increase in price so, if income elasticity=2, quantity demanded has risen by $2 \times 4\% = 8\%$.

So D.

Solution 29

Government intervention is not a feature of a free market since this market is determined by consumers and producers.

So D.

Solution 30

C.

Solution 31

A natural barrier to entry is one which happens through economic forces, e.g. economies of scale. Alternatives B, C and D are all barriers created by governments.

So A.

Solution 32

In perfect competition and monopolistic competition, there are no barriers to entry.

So D.

Solution 33

One of the most prevalent features of all imperfect markets is excess capacity. This happens because the profit maximising output is reached when the average cost curve is still falling.

So C.

Solution 34

In a cartel, it is the cartel which sets both price and output.

So A.

Solution 35

The expenditure method of measuring national income measures economic activity by summing the value of expenditure on final goods.

So B.

Solution 36

Net national product is equal to gross domestic product + net property income from abroad less depreciation.

So D.

Solution 37

Equilibrium will take place where $Y = \text{AD}$ and in a closed economy, this is where

So:

$$Y = C + 1 + G$$

$$Y = 0.8\,(Y - T) + 1 + G$$

$$= 0.2Y = 1 + G - 0.8T$$

So:

$$Y = 5(1 + G) - 4T$$

If G and T are reduced by 100:

$$Y = 0.8(Y - (T - 100) + 1 + (G - 100)$$

So:

$$Y = 5(1 + G) - 4T - 100$$

So C.

Solution 38

A world recession is likely to lead to a leftward shift in a country's macroeconomic demand schedule.

So A.

Solution 39

We need to convert £600m into 20X8 prices, so:

$$£600\text{m} \times \frac{100}{120} = £500\text{m}$$

So, in real terms, the economy between 20X8 and 20X9 remained the same.

So D.

Solution 40

In order to calculate a question like this, we can either add the value on at each stage or take the value of the final product. The latter is easier.

So:		
	Firm B is worth	£400
	Firm C is worth	£600
	Firm A is not included	
		£1,000

So C.

Solution 41

The short-run aggregate supply curve is positively sloped because, with given input prices, firms' unit costs rise with output.

So B.

Solution 42

In the short run, there will be some increase in GDP and some in prices but in the long run, there will be higher prices but no increase in GDP.

So B.

Solution 43

The statement which is incorrect is that a current account deficit is a sign of weakness, while a surplus is a sign of strength.

So C.

Solution 44

This is a supply side issue, so reductions in income tax would increase the incentive to work.

So C.

Solution 45

The aggregate demand curve is negatively sloped because consumer spending falls at higher price levels owing to the fall in the real value of their savings, and net exports fall as domestic goods' prices rise relative to foreign prices.

So D.

Solution 46

Similar to Question 40.

From B £1,400 + Firm C £2,200 = £3,600.

So B.

Solution 47

The balance of payments itself must balance. A surplus will be reflected in an inflow of currency and reserves, a deficit will show an outflow.

So D.

Solution 48

The principle of comparative advantage is that by specialising in production of goods which can be made relatively cheaply and trading with others who specialise in producing different products, all can become better off.

So A.

Solution 49

Final goods are goods which are purchased by the ultimate user.

So C.

Solution 50

The average propensity to consume may be defined as the level of consumption divided by the level of disposable income.

So B.

Solution 51

In order to be counted as part of national income, there must be an expenditure, an output and an income which would include a housekeeper's salary and the pay of a fire officer but not child allowance.

So (ii) and (iii) – Answer B.

Solution 52

The accelerator principle states that an increase in consumer demand leads to a more than proportionate increase in the level of investment.

So B.

Solution 53

Household saving is equal to disposable income less consumption expenditure.

So D.

Solution 54

$$\text{MPC} = \frac{1{,}500}{6{,}000} = 0.25$$

$$\text{Multiplier} = \frac{1}{1 - 0.25} = \frac{1}{0.75}$$

$$= 1.33$$

So answer = A.

Solution 55

Alternatives A, B and C are all withdrawals, government expenditure is an injection, so an increase in G would cause real GDP to rise.

So D.

Solution 56

The difference in the shape of the short-run and the long-run aggregate supply curve can be explained by the assumption that wage constraints are fixed in the long run.

So D.

Solution 57

Residual error is found in output and income method, since expenditure method is deemed to be more reliable.

So B – (i) and (iii).

Solution 58

According to Keynes, transactions demand for money is a function of income and speculative demand is a function of interest rates.

So C.

Solution 59

Venture capital is similar to share capital in that it is a long-term liability.

So C.

Solution 60

The money market is concerned with short-term finance, the capital market is concerned with the long term. So answer is banks and discount houses.

So A – (i) and (ii).

Solution 61

Where shares are falling or underperforming, this is known as a bear market.

So B.

Solution 62

If you are receiving a £5 rate of return on a £95 investment, this equates to approximately 5.26% over 3 months. So the approximate annual rate is 5.26% × 4 = 21.04%.

This makes alternative D the closest.

Solution 63

If the government wants to avoid recession, it should lower interest rates to encourage investment and lower the reserve asset ratio to give banks more liquidity.

So B.

Solution 64

The purchasing power parity path is the path of the nominal exchange rate that would keep the real exchange rate constant.

So D.

Solution 65

A sudden discrete fall in the fixed exchange rate which the government commits itself to defend is called a devaluation.

So C.

✓ Solution 66

Take a simple numerical example where both Good X and Good Y are £10 each. If X rises by 40%, it will now cost £14. If Y falls by 30%, it will now cost £7. So, for country A – terms of trade have gone from $\frac{10}{10}$ to $\frac{14}{7}$ an improvement of 100%.

So C.

✓ Solution 67

In the short term the exchange rate will fall but, in the long term, it should revert back to its purchasing parity.

So D.

✓ Solution 68

Monetarists believe that in the long term, unemployment can be reduced by increasing efficiency and productivity.

So C.

✓ Solution 69

A country has an absolute advantage if it can produce a good or service using fewer resources, it has a comparative advantage if it has a lower opportunity cost. In country C opportunity is half a unit of V, in country D opportunity cost is one and a half units.

So B.

✓ Solution 70

If current account is in deficit by £7bn and capital account is in surplus of £4bn, overall deficit is £3bn. If we sell reserves of £2bn, there is still shortfall of £1bn which we could borrow from IMF.

So B.

✓ Solution 71

Of the alternatives given, only fiscal policy is more effective since interest rates are pegged to international levels ensuring that crowding out does not happen.

So D.

✓ Solution 72

Given that the terms of trade index is:

$$\frac{\text{P index of exports}}{\text{PI index of imports}} \times 100$$

Statement (i) is false
Statement (ii) could be true
Statement (iii) is true

So answer D.

Solution 73

A reversal of Question 72:
Statement (i) is false
Statement (ii) could be true
Statement (iii) is true

So, answer D.

Solution 74

Current a/c	– £17bn
Capital a/c	+ £8bn
Sales of reserves	+ £2bn
Shortfall of	£7bn

So B.

Solution 75

The Marshall – Lerner condition states that for a devaluation to work the combined sum of the price elasticities of demand for exports and imports must be greater than 1.

So C.

Mock Assessment 3

Paper C04
Fundamentals of Business Economics

Instructions: attempt all 75 questions

Time allowed 2 hours

Do not turn the page until you are ready to attempt the assessment under timed conditions

Mock Assessment – Questions

? Question 1

A scarce resource is one for which:

(A) There is a high opportunity cost
(B) The demand at a zero price would exceed the available supply
(C) Demand always exceeds supply
(D) The world has a finite supply

? Question 2

The rewards for capital and enterprise are:

(A) Land and labour
(B) Capital and labour
(C) Interest and profit
(D) Rent and wages

? Question 3

Which of the following is the best example of a social cost?

(A) Road congestion
(B) Health
(C) Education
(D) Street lighting

? Question 4

An economy is described as efficient if:

(A) There is full employment
(B) GDP is rising each year
(C) There is a balance of payments surplus
(D) It can only produce more of one good by producing less of another

? Question 5

Which of the following are used to measure how the public sector performs?

(i) Economy
(ii) Efficiency
(iii) Effectiveness
(iv) Extravagance

(A) (i), (ii)
(B) (ii), (iii)
(C) (iii), (iv)
(D) (i), (ii), (iii)

Question 6

The type of business in which a public company is engaged in is determined by:

(A) Articles of Association
(B) Memorandum of Association
(C) Certificate of Incorporation
(D) Share Capital

Questions 7 – 10 are based on the following data:

Quantity	Price	Total Cost
0	-	200
1	200	250
2	180	300
3	160	350
4	140	400
5	120	450
6	100	500

Question 7

The average fixed cost of producing 5 units is:

(A) £40
(B) £50
(C) £100
(D) £200

Question 8

At what output is profit maximised?

(A) 3
(B) 4
(C) 5
(D) 6

Question 9

Price elasticity of demand between 5 and 6 units is:

(A) Elastic
(B) Inelastic
(C) Unity Elasticity
(D) Impossible to determine

Question 10

The marginal cost of the second unit is:

(A) £50
(B) £150
(C) £200
(D) £250

Questions 11 – 15 are based on the following scenario:

Company X PLC	
Share price beginning of the year	£1.20
Share price end of the year	£1.50
Dividend paid	12 pence per share
Net profit before and after taxation	£25,000 and £20,000
No. of ordinary shares	100,000
Interest paid	£10,000

Question 11

The dividend yield was:

(A) 7.5%
(B) 10%
(C) 12%
(D) 14%

Question 12

The dividend cover is:

(A) 1.25
(B) 1.5
(C) 1.666
(D) 2.5

Question 13

The interest cover was:

(A) 1
(B) 2
(C) 3
(D) 4

Question 14

The earnings per share was:

(A) 5p
(B) 10p
(C) 15p
(D) 20p

Question 15

The price/earnings ratio is:

(A) 2.5
(B) 5
(C) 7.5
(D) 10

Question 16

The first attempt at reviewing corporate governance in the U.K. was the setting up of:

(A) The Cadbury Committee
(B) The Greenbury Committe
(C) The Nolan Committee
(D) The Higgs Committee

Question 17

Which of the following is not a good feature of corporate governance?

(A) A board which comprises executive and non-executive directors
(B) Adoption of transparency, openness and fairness
(C) A board of directors who are fully accountable
(D) An individual who holds the position of Chief Executive and Chairman

Question 18

Non-Executive Directors are appointed by:

(A) Shareholders
(B) The External Auditor
(C) The Chief Executive
(D) The Board of Directors

Question 19

Which of the following events would shift the demand curve for Good X o the left?

(A) An increase in consumers' income
(B) An increase in the price of Good X
(C) An increase in the price of a substitute good
(D) An increase in the price of a complementary good

Question 20

If price is reduced from £10 to £9 and demand rises from 100 units to 120 units, then price elasticity of demand is:

(A) –1
(B) +1
(C) –2
(D) +2

Question 21

If income rises from £450 to £500 but we reduce our expenditure on bus travel, this implies:

(A) Bus travel is a normal good
(B) Bus travel is a necessity
(C) Bus travel is an inferior good
(D) Bus travel is a giffen good

Question 22

If cross elasticity of demand is –1 between two products, this would indicate:

(A) They are perfect substitutes
(B) They are perfect complements
(C) Both are inferior goods
(D) Both are Giffen goods

Question 23

Which one of the following will shift the supply curve for Good X to the right?

(A) A government subsidy in the production of Good X
(B) A decrease in labour productivity in the production of Good X
(C) An increase in the price of materials used to produce Good X
(D) An increase in real wages paid to producers of Good X

Question 24

A baker produces 100 loaves of bread for £1.50 per loaf. If the price of bread rises to £1.65 and the baker increases his production to 120 loaves, the elasticity of supply is:

(A) –1
(B) –2
(C) +1
(D) +2

Question 25

The time taken to adjust one factor of production is known as:

(A) The short-run
(B) The long-run
(C) The medium term
(D) None of the above

Question 26

A minimum price is set for Good X at £10 which is below market price. A decrease in the supply of Good X keeping the minimum price fixed at £10 will result in:

(A) A rise in price and a surplus of Good X
(B) A rise in price and a shortage of Good X

(C) No change in price and a shortage of Good X
(D) A rise in price and a balance between supply and demand for Good X

Question 27

If the government set a maximum price below the market equilibrium price, this will lead to:

(A) Excess demand
(B) Excess supply
(C) Market equilibrium
(D) None of the above

Question 28

A business employs 10 workers at a wage rate of £450. To attract one more worker, the wage rate is increased to £475. What is the marginal cost of the 11th worker?

(A) 475
(B) 525
(C) 725
(D) 825

Question 29

Which of the following is not a reason why economies of scale may exist?

(A) Indivisibilities
(B) Division of labour
(C) Physical facors
(D) Increase in technology over time

Question 30

A fixed factor of production:

(A) Cannot be sold in the short-run
(B) Cannot be moved in the short-run
(C) Cannot have its input level varied in the short-run
(D) Cannot have its input level varied

Question 31

If Tesco plc acquired an airline, this would be an example of:

(A) Horizontal integration
(B) Vertical integration upwards
(C) Vertical integration backwards
(D) Conglomerate diversification

Question 32

Which one of the following is the best example of an artificial barrier to entry?

(A) Patent
(B) Economies of scale
(C) High entry costs
(D) Branding

Question 33

Which one of the following is not compatible with perfect competition?

(A) Marginal Cost = Marginal Revenue
(B) Marginal Cost = Average Cost
(C) Marginal Cost = Price
(D) Marginal Revenue = 0

Question 34

Which of the following is not a feature of monopolistic competition?

(A) Normal profit
(B) Excess capacity
(C) Many buyers and sellers
(D) Price discrimination

Question 35

Which of the following is illegal in the U.K.?

(A) Predatory pricing
(B) Advertising
(C) Cartels
(D) Mergers

Question 36

A contestable market is one where:

(A) Firms bid against each other for a contract
(B) Entry and exit from the market is cheap and easy
(C) The utilities are regulated
(D) There is a high degree of failure

Question 37

A good which is characterised by both rivalry and excludability is known as:

(A) A merit good
(B) A public good
(C) A private good
(D) None of the above

Question 38

If the reserve asset ratio was 40%, how much money could a bank create from an initial deposit of £1,000?

(A) £2,000
(B) £2,500
(C) £4,000
(D) £10,000

Question 39

Speculative demand for money is a function of:

(A) Wealth
(B) Savings
(C) Income
(D) Interest rates

Question 40

If the normal rate of interest is 5% and the rate of inflation is 8%, then the real rate of interest is:

(A) 5%
(B) 7%
(C) –3%
(D) –2%

Question 41

Which of the following markets are run by the Stock Exchange?

(i) Gilt-edged
(ii) U.K. Fully Listed Securities
(iii) Alternative Investment Market
(iv) Overseas Securities

(A) (i), (ii)
(B) (i), (ii), (iii)
(C) (i), (ii), (iv)
(D) (i), (ii), (iii), (iv)

Question 42

What is/are the difference(s) between an investment trust and a unit trust?

(i) A unit trust is a trust in the legal sense
(ii) In a unit trust money raised comes only from investors
(iii) A unit trust is only allowed to undertake certain investments

(A) (i) only
(B) (i), (ii)

(C) (ii), (iii)
(D) (i), (ii), (iii)

? Question 43

Which of the following would be regarded as long-term capital?

(i) Ordinary shares
(ii) Debentures
(iii) Convertible bond

(A) (i) only
(B) (i), (ii)
(C) (ii), (iii)
(D) (i), (ii), (iii)

? Question 44

If money supply is £200 million, velocity of circulation is 5, transactions demand £250 million, what is the average price level?

(A) 3
(B) 4
(C) 5
(D) 6

? Question 45

If the central bank was to increase interest rates, what would be the least likely economic consequence?

(A) The exchange rate would rise
(B) The price of non-financial assets would fall
(C) Inflation should fall
(D) Consumer expenditure would rise

? Question 46

Which of the following statements is true?

(A) According to the Keynesians savings is determined by income, according to the monetarists savings is determined by interest rates
(B) The Keynesians believe savings are determined by interest rates, so do the monetarists
(C) The Keynesians believe savings are determined by interest rates, the monetarists believe savings is determined by inome
(D) Keynesians and monetarists believe savings is determined by the Marginal Efficiency of Capital

Question 47

Which of the following financial institutions belongs to the money market?

(A) The Discount Market
(B) The Stock Exchange
(C) Lloyds of London
(D) Unit and Investment Trusts

Questions 48 – 50 are based on the following information:

	Market Prices £bn
Consumers expenditure	£250
General government final consumption	£100
Gross domestic fixed capital formation	£75
Value of increase in stocks and WIP	£25
Exports	£50
Imports	£55
Net property income from abroad	£5
Taxes	£130
Subsidies	£20
Capital consumption	£25

Question 48

Gross Domestic Product at market prices is:

(A) £400bn
(B) £425bn
(C) £450bn
(D) £475bn

Question 49

Gross National Product at market prices is:

(A) £410bn
(B) £420bn
(C) £430bn
(D) £435bn

Question 50

Net National Product at factor cost is:

(A) £260bn
(B) £275bn
(C) £290bn
(D) £310bn

Question 51

Which of the following are transfer payments?

(i) Pension
(ii) Family allowance
(iii) Lecturer's salary
(iv) Payment made to babysitter

(A) (i), (ii)
(B) (i), (ii), (iii)
(C) (i), (ii), (iv)
(D) (i), (ii), (iii), (iv)

Question 52

The marginal propensity to consume is equal to:

(A) Change in C/change in Y
(B) Change in C/actual Y
(C) Actual C/actual Y
(D) Actual c/change in Y

Question 53

In a given economy of each additional £1 of income 20% is taken in taxes, 10% spent on imports and 10% is saved. The value of the multiplier is:

(A) 1
(B) 2
(C) 2.5
(D) 2.67

Question 54

A closed economy with no government sector has a marginal propensity to consume of 0.8 and a full employment level of £125m. The current level of income is £100m. To achieve full employment, how much must investment rise?

(A) £2m
(B) £4m
(C) £5m
(D) £10m

Question 55

Which of the following would cause a leakage from the circular flow?

(i) Increase in imports
(ii) Increase in taxes
(iii) Reduction in government expenditure

(A) (i)
(B) (i), (ii)
(C) (i), (iii)
(D) (i), (ii), (iii)

Question 56

Who are the gainers from inflation?

(i) Borrowers
(ii) Savers
(iii) Those who hold cash
(iii) Those who invest in assets

(A) (i), (ii)
(B) (i), (iii)
(C) (ii), (iii)
(D) (i), (iv)

Question 57

During the 20th century in the U.K., workers lost their jobs in the coal and steel industries. This is an example of which type of unemployment?

(A) Cyclical
(B) Structural
(C) Seasonal
(D) Frictional

Question 58

Which of the following is not an example of supply side economics?

(A) Privatisation
(B) Lower state benefits
(C) Lower direct taxes
(D) Increased government expenditure

Question 59

Value Added Tax is an expenditure tax which is:

(A) Progressive and direct
(B) Progressive and indirect
(C) Regressive and indirect
(D) Regressive and direct

Question 60

Which of the following are included in Adam Smith's "Canons of Taxation"?

(i) Certainty
(ii) Convenience
(iii) Corporation
(iv) Customs

(A) (i), (ii)
(B) (i), (iii)
(C) (i), (iii), (iv)
(D) (i), (ii), (iii), (iv)

Question 61

If the government wishes to pursue a contractionary fiscal policy, it should:

(A) Increase taxes, increase government expenditure
(B) Increase taxes, reduce government expenditure
(C) Reduce taxes, reduce government expenditure
(D) Reduce taxes, increase government expenditure

Question 62

Which of the following is not a direct tax?

(A) Income Tax
(B) Corporation Tax
(C) National Insurance
(D) Customs and Excise

Question 63

If the government want to maximise the amount of tax raised on a good, they should choose one where:

(A) Demand is inelastic, supply is inelastic
(B) Demand is elastic, supply is inelastic
(C) Demand is inelastic, supply is elastic
(D) Demand is elastic, supply is elastic

Question 64

Which of the following are examples of government non-marketable debt?

(i) Treasury Bills
(ii) Gilt-edged Stocks
(iii) National Savings Certificates
(iv) Premium Bonds

(A) (i), (ii)
(B) (i), (iii)
(C) (ii), (iv)
(D) (iii), (iv)

Question 65

	2009	2010
Export Index	100	113.8
Import Index	100	105.2

The terms of trade for 2010 were:

(A) .92
(B) 1.00
(C) 1.08
(D) 1.86

Question 66

The theory of comparative advantage was formulated by:

(A) Adam Smith
(B) David Riccardo
(C) John Maynard Keynes
(D) Gordon Brown

Question 67

Which of the following are examples of protectionism?

(i) Import quota
(ii) Import tariff
(iii) Export subsidy

(A) (i) only
(B) (i), (ii)
(C) (ii), (iii)
(D) (i), (ii) and (iii)

Question 68

The purchasing power parity path is:

(A) The path that economists think that a currency will always follow
(B) The path that the domestic money supply must follow to keep price at the world level
(C) The path of the real exchange rate that would keep the nominal exchange rate constant
(D) The path of the nominal exchange rate that would keep the real exchange rate constant

Question 69

If a country's terms of trade index falls, this means that:

(i) Export prices have risen faster than import prices
(ii) Import prices have risen faster than export prices
(iii) The balance of trade is in deficit

(A) (i) and (ii)
(B) (ii) and (iii)
(C) (i) only
(D) (ii) only

Questions 70 – 72 are based on the following data:

Exports	£20 million
Imports	£23 million
Invisible surplus	£2 million
Capital A/C	£5 million inflow

Question 70

The visible trade balance was:

(A) £3m surplus
(B) £3m deficit
(C) £5m surplus
(D) £5m deficit

Question 71

The current account balance was:

(A) £1m surplus
(B) £1m deficit
(C) £5m surplus
(D) £5m deficit

Question 72

The Balance of Payments was:

(A) – £4m
(B) + £4m
(C) – £7m
(D) + £7m

Question 73

The absolute loss of jobs in the manufacturing sector of an economy is known as:

(A) Deindustrialisation
(B) Devaluation
(C) Post Industrialisation
(D) None of the above

Question 74

An American imported car cost £100,000 last year in the U.K. when the sterling/dollar exchange rate is now £1 = $1.50 and the dollar price has risen by 10%. What is the sterling price of this car today?

(A) £150,000
(B) £146,666
(C) £120,000
(D) £100,000

Question 75

An individual now pays more tax because his income has risen and it pushes him into a higher tax bracket. This is known as:

(A) Fiscal Stance
(B) Fisca Drag
(C) Fiscal Instability
(D) None of the above

Mock Assessment – Answers

✓ Solution 1

The economic definition is the demand at a zero price would exceed the available supply.

So B.

✓ Solution 2

The rewards for capital and enterprise are interest and profit.

So C

✓ Solution 3

B and C are merit goods. D is a public good.

So A.

✓ Solution 4

An economy is described as efficient if it can only produce more of one good by producing less of another.

So D.

✓ Solution 5

Public sector performance is based on the 3 Es – economy, efficiency and effectiveness.

So D.

✓ Solution 6

The Memorandum of Association tells us what type of business a public company is engaged in.

So B.

✓ Solution 7

Fixed Cost = 200 Total Cost at 0 output

$$AFC = \frac{200}{5} = 40$$

So A.

Solution 8

Output	Profit
3	130
4	160
5	150
6	100

So B.

Solution 9

Answer C – unity elasticity because total revenue does not change.

Solution 10

Total Cost at 1	250
Total Cost at 2	300
Difference	£50

So A.

Solution 11

Dividend yield

= Share price beginning of year £1.20

Dividend paid 12p

= 10%

So B.

Solution 12

Profit after tax 20,000 = 1.666

Dividend paid 12,000

So C.

Solution 13

$$\frac{\text{Net profit before interest and tax}}{\text{Interest paid}} = \frac{30,000}{10,000}$$

= 3

So C.

Solution 14

Earnings per share $= \frac{£20,000}{100,000}$

$= 20p$

So D.

Solution 15

P E ratio $= \frac{£1.50}{20p}$ 7.5

So C.

Solution 16

The first attempt at reviewing corporate governance in the U.K. was the setting up of The Cadbury Committee.

So D.

Solution 17

An individual who holds the position of Chief Executive and Chairman is not a good feature of corporate governance.

So D.

Solution 18

Non-Executive Directors are appointed by The Board of Directors.

So D.

Solution 19

A shift in the demand curve to the left represents a fall in demand. This could be caused by a rise in the price of a complementary good.

So D.

Solution 20

$\frac{\text{\% change in QD}}{\text{\% change in price}} \quad \frac{20}{-10} = -2$

So C.

Solution 21

A negative income elasticity of demand implies that bus travel is an inferior good.

So C.

Solution 22

If cross elasticity of demand is –1, this would indicate that the two goods in question are perfect complements.

So B.

Solution 23

A government subsidy would shift the supply curve to the right since it makes the product cheaper.

So A.

Solution 24

% change in QS	+ 20	=	2
% change in price	+ 10		

So D.

Solution 25

The time taken to adjust one factor of production is known as the short-run.

So A.

Solution 26

A rise in price and a balance between supply and demand for Good X.

So D.

Solution 27

If the government set a maximum price below the market equilibrium price, this will lead to excess demand.

So A.

Solution 28

475	11th wage
250	extra £25 each of 1st ten
725	

So C.

Solution 29

Economies of scale refer to changes in the scale of production, not the time scale.

So D.

Solution 30

A fixed factor of production cannot have its output level varied in the short term.

So C.

Solution 31

This is an example of conglomerate diversification, moving into an entirely different industry.

So D.

Solution 32

An artificial barrier to entry is created by the government so patent.

Answer A.

Solution 33

Since, under perfect competition marginal revenue = price, alternative D is not compatible.

Solution 34

Price discrimination can only take place when you can control supply.

So D.

Solution 35

It is illegal to form a cartel in the U.K.

So C.

Solution 36

A contestable market is one where entry and exit from the market is cheap and easy.

So B.

Solution 37

A good which is characterised by both rivalry and excludability is known as a private good.

So C.

Solution 38

$$\frac{1}{.4} = 2.5 \times £1{,}000$$

= £2,500.

So B.

Solution 39

Speculative demand for money is a function of interest rates.

So D.

Solution 40

Nominal rate of interest		5%
less rate of inflation		– 8%
	so	– 3%

Answer C.

Solution 41

The Gilt-edged, U.K. Fully Listed Securities, Alternative Investment Market and Overseas Securities are all markets run by the Stock Exchange.

So D.

Solution 42

A unit trust is a trust in the legal sense.
In a unit trust money raised only comes from investors.
A unit trust is only allowed to undertake certain investments.

So D.

Solution 43

Ordinary shares, debentures and convertible bonds are all examples of long-term capital.

So D.

Solution 44

£200m	250m
x 5	x ?
= £1,000,000	= £1,000,000

Answer 4 – So B.

Solution 45

If the central bank was to increase interest rates, consumer expenditure would fall.

So B.

Solution 46

Keynesians believe that savings are determined by income, monetarists would say savings are determined by interest rates.

So A.

Solution 47

The discount market belongs to the money market. The Stock Exchange, Unit and Investment Trusts belong to the capital market. Lloyds of London is an insurance market.

So A.

Solution 48

	£bn
Consumers expenditure	£250
General government final consumption	£100
Gross domestic fixed capital formation	£75
Value of increase in stocks and WIP	£25
Exports	£50
Imports	(£55)
	£425bn

Answer B.

Solution 49

£425bn + £5bn = £430bn

So C.

Solution 50

£425bn
(£130)bn
£20bn
(£25)bn
£290bn

So C.

Solution 51

Pensions and family allowance are transfer payments, i.e. income not earned.

So A.

Solution 52

The marginal propensity to consume is equal to change in C/change in Y.

So A.

Solution 53

$$\text{Multiplier} = \frac{1}{\text{mpw}}$$

$$= \frac{1}{.2 + .1 + .1} = \frac{1}{.4} = 2.5$$

So C.

Solution 54

If mpc = .8
Multiplier = 5
If income needs to rise by £25m
£5m × 5 = £25m.

So C.

Solution 55

An increase in imports, an increase in taxes and a reduction in government expenditure would all constitute a leakage from the circular flow of income.

So D.

Solution 56

Borrowers and those who hold assets gain from inflation.

So D.

Solution 57

This was caused by changes in the structure of industry.

So B.

Solution 58

Increasing government expenditure changes demand not supply.

So D.

Solution 59

An expenditure tax is indirect and regressive.

So C.

Solution 60

The four canons of taxation are certainty, convenience, equitable and economy.

So A.

Solution 61

If the government wishes to pursue a contractionary fiscal policy, it should increase taxes and reduce government expenditure.

So C.

Solution 62

Customs and Excise is an expenditure tax.

So D.

Solution 63

If the government was to maximise the amount of tax raised on a good, they want both demand and supply to be inelastic.

So C.

Solution 64

National Savings Certificates and Premium Bonds are examples of government non-marketable debt.

So D.

Solution 65

Terms of trade for 2010:

$$\frac{113.8}{105.2}$$

So C.

Solution 66

The theory of comparative advantage was formulated by David Riccardo.

So B.

Solution 67

Import quotas, import tariffs and export subsidies are all examples of protectionism.

So D.

Solution 68

The purchasing power parity path is the path of the nominal exchange rate that would keep the real exchange rate constant.

So D.

Solution 69

If a country's terms of trade index falls, this means that import prices have risen faster than export prices.

So D.

Solution 70

Exports	£20 million
Imports	£23 million
	£3 million deficit

So B.

Solution 71

The current account balance was:

Visible	– £3m
Invisible	+ £2m
	– £1m

So B.

Solution 72

Current a/c	– £1m
Capital a/c	+ £5m
	+ £4m

So B.

Solution 73

The absolute loss of jobs in the manufacturing sector of an economy is known as deindustrialisation.

So A.

Solution 74

At £1 = $2 dollar price was $200,000, if dollar price has risen by 10% it is now $220,000. At an exchange rate of £1 = $1.50 sterling price is now

$$£146,666 = \frac{\$220,000}{1.5}$$

So B.

Solution 75

An individual forced to pay more tax caused by a rise in income moving them into a higher tax bracket is known as fiscal drag.

So B.